A Short Literary History of the United States

A Short Literary History of the United States offers an introduction to American Literature for students who want to acquaint themselves with the most important periods, authors, and works of American literary history. Comprehensive yet concise, it provides an essential overview of the different currents in American literature in an accessible, engaging style. This book features:

- the precolonial era to the present, including new media formats
- the evolution of literary traditions, themes, and aesthetics
- overviews and comparisons of individual authors
- readings of individual texts, contextualized within American cultural history
- literary theory in the United States
- a core reading list in American Literature
- a glossary of key terms.

This book is ideal as a companion to courses in American Literature and American Studies, or as a study aid for exams.

Mario Klarer is Professor and Chair of the Department of American Studies at the University of Innsbruck, Austria.

A Short Literary History of the United States

Mario Klarer

LONDON AND NEW YORK

Published 2013
by C.H. Beck, Munich
as *Literaturgeschichte der USA*

This edition published 2014
by Routledge
2 Park Square, Milton Park, Abingdon, Oxon OX14 4RN

and by Routledge
711 Third Avenue, New York, NY 10017

Routledge is an imprint of the Taylor & Francis Group, an informa business

© 2013, 2014 Mario Klarer

The right of Mario Klarer to be identified as author of this work has been asserted by him in accordance with sections 77 and 78 of the Copyright, Designs and Patents Act 1988.

All rights reserved. No part of this book may be reprinted or reproduced or utilised in any form or by any electronic, mechanical, or other means, now known or hereafter invented, including photocopying and recording, or in any information storage or retrieval system, without permission in writing from the publishers.

Trademark notice: Product or corporate names may be trademarks or registered trademarks, and are used only for identification and explanation without intent to infringe.

British Library Cataloguing in Publication Data
A catalogue record for this book is available from the British Library

Library of Congress Cataloging in Publication Data
Klarer, Mario, 1962–
  A Short Literary History of the United States/Mario Klarer.
  Includes bibliographical references and index.
  1. American literature – History and criticism. I. Title.
  PS92.K57 2014
  810.9 – dc23
  2013043369

ISBN: 978-0-415-74215-3 (hbk)
ISBN: 978-0-415-74217-7 (pbk)
ISBN: 978-1-315-78011-5 (ebk)

Typeset in Bembo
by Florence Production, Stoodleigh, Devon, UK

For Bernadette, Johanna,
and Moritz

Contents

List of figures	ix
Introduction	xi
1 Discovery narratives	1
2 Colonial literature	10
3 Literature of the Early Republic	27
4 Transcendentalism	37
5 American Renaissance	44
6 Gilded Age – Realism	60
7 Modernism	70
8 Postmodernism	93
9 Ethnic voices	106
10 Literary theory in the United States	112
Extended glossary and study aid	132
Suggested further reading	162
Bibliography	178
Author and title index	181
Subject index	193

Figures

1.1	Woodcut from 1505, regarded as one of the earliest depictions of Native Americans. Photo by James Whitmore. Time Life Pictures/Getty Images	2
1.2	"America," engraving by Theodor Galle (1571–1633) after a drawing by Jan van der Straet (Stradanus, 1523–1604). © De Agostini/The British Library Board	3
1.3	Woodcut depicting a scene from Amerigo Vespucci's voyages from the 1509 Strasbourg edition of his *Letter to Pier Soderini*	4
1.4	Watercolor painting by John White depicting an Inuit man. © The Trustees of the British Museum	8
2.1	Engraving by Theodor de Bry, based on the work of John White, from Harriot's *Brief and True Report of the New-Found Land of Virginia* (1588) depicting a Native American. © The British Library Board	11
2.2	Title page of the 1773 edition of Mary Rowlandson's *A True History of the Captivity and Restoration of Mrs. Mary Rowlandson*	16
2.3	Title page of Phillis Wheatley's *Poems on Various Subjects* (1773)	25
3.1	List of thirteen virtues for each day of the week from *The Autobiography of Benjamin Franklin* (1771–1790)	30
3.2	Neoclassical villa of Monticello, designed by Thomas Jefferson, photograph by Moritz Klarer	31
4.1	Map of Walden Pond (1846) from Henry David Thoreau's *Walden* (1854). © The Walden Woods Project	39

5.1	Portrait of Walt Whitman (1854) by Samuel Hollyer of a daguerreotype by Gabriel Harrison, frontispiece of the first edition of *Leaves of Grass* (1855). © Courtesy of Bayley/Whitman Collection of Ohio Wesleyan University	53
6.1	Illustration by Edward Winsor Kemble for the first edition of *Huckleberry Finn* (1884)	62
7.1	Portrait of Gertrude Stein (1906) by Pablo Picasso. © 2011 Estate of Pablo Picasso/Artists Rights Society (ARS) New York	72
7.2	Movie poster for *Temptation* (1936), directed by Oscar Micheaux. Photograph by John D. Kisch/Separate Cinema Archive/Getty Images	86
8.1	Self-portrait in a convex mirror (*c.*1523–1524) by Parmigianino	97
8.2	Thomas Pynchon's 2004 appearance in *The Simpsons* (season 15, episode 10)	101
9.1	DVD cover of *The Wire* (season 1). Courtesy of HBO	109

Introduction

Although we can only talk about the United States of America after the Declaration of Independence by the North American colonies in 1776, this *Short Literary History of the United States* consciously transcends this time line. Only when taking into account the older literary production in the North American territories and colonies before the formation of the United States is it possible to shed light on the historical dimension of its literary tradition.

This overview of American literature begins with early accounts of discovery and travel. Although these first documents differentiate little between geographic regions, mostly addressing the New World as a whole, nevertheless, they anticipate tendencies of the later image of America in general and the image of the United States in particular. Subsequent colonial literature on the east coast of the North American continent early on produces regional facets of what will become United States literature. The texts of the Early Republic will later instrumentalize these elements to define a national identity in contrast to English literature. Transcendentalism and the American Renaissance of the nineteenth century push this rhetoric even further by advocating an autochthonous, idiosyncratically American literature. Like a leitmotif, these achievements of an independent tradition fuel the subsequent periods of the Gilded Age before the turn of the century, as well as modernism in the first half of the twentieth century. Even authors after World War II, including the Beat Generation and the postmodernists, keep referring back to this first indigenous American literary movement associated with the transcendentalists. In the latter part of the twentieth century, a growing chorus of ethnic voices from *within* the United States questions this long-standing American literary identity, which largely derived its legitimacy by claiming American achievements in contrast to English or European influences.

This short literary history attempts to trace American literature from its beginning in the early modern image of the New World during the Age of Discovery to the contemporary literary landscape of the early twenty-first century. The book discusses all major periods by selecting representative texts of central authors in order to pinpoint their paradigmatic character and innovative potential for the tradition of American literature. In order to make the text useful for beginners in literary studies, the book is deliberately short, thereby guaranteeing an unobstructed overview of major trends, authors, and texts, without running the risk of confusing readers with too much detail. A chapter on literary theory in the United States provides a first overview of the methodological questions concerning American literature as well as larger theoretical trends in the humanities in general. A concise glossary with the most important terms pertinent to American literature rounds out the book as a potential self-study guide. The book should therefore be an ideal companion to introductory classes in English or American literature, giving the student a first comprehensive overview of *all* of American literature, before advancing to more focused and specialized courses.

In Chapters 1 through 9 the names of the major authors are rendered in bold typeface in order to facilitate easy orientation for the user. The same principle also applies to major movements in literary theory throughout Chapter 10.

The final work on the English translation of this book was completed at the National Humanities Center in North Carolina in a fruitful exchange with the research fellows of the class of 2012–2013. Geoffrey Galt Harpham, Director, and Elizabeth Mansfield, Vice President for Scholarly Programs, made this year possible. I am indebted to the staff of the Center for their support, including the excellent suggestions by Karen Carroll. Thanks also go to my colleagues at the American Studies Department at the University of Innsbruck in Austria: Sonja Bahn, Saskia Fürst, Gudrun Grabher, Roberta Hofer, Cornelia Klecker,

Johannes Mahlknecht, Christian Quendler, and Christian Stenico. Monika Datterl has made indispensable contributions to the manuscript in all its different stages and guided the text through the final steps of the publication process. My greatest thanks once again go to my wife Bernadette Rangger for critically discussing all of the chapters with me and for providing everything else to make our family life wonderful.

Mario Klarer

1 Discovery narratives

The most important cultural and historical impetus for the development of literature in and about America is, of course, the discovery of the New World in the fifteenth and sixteenth centuries. What seems obvious at first glance proves to be far more complex on closer inspection, since preconceived notions of America had existed in the European imagination long before the actual discovery of the new continent. Here, it is important to examine the background of Columbus's discovery. The reason for his voyage was to find a new sea passage to India. Instead of going around the Cape of Good Hope eastward, Columbus embarked on a westward journey around the world. This route to the Far East via the West made it possible to fuse existing ideas concerning both hemispheres, the East and the West, into one composite image of America.

Greco-Roman and medieval texts had anchored the Far East of Asia and the extreme West of the Atlantic as utopian places in the European imagination. In the fourth century BC, for example, Plato described the fabled state of Atlantis as situated in the ocean beyond the Pillars of Hercules, the entrance to the Strait of Gibraltar. During the Middle Ages, fantastical travel reports, as, for example, by the Irish monk St. Brendan, continued these westward projections in descriptions of miraculous islands in the Atlantic. Parallel to an imaginary West, Judeo-Christian belief had located the earthly paradise in the East of Asia. In the Middle Ages, travel reports by Marco Polo and by the fantastical John Mandeville fueled and concretized this tradition of a paradisiacal Far East.

2 *Discovery narratives*

The moment that **Christopher Columbus** (1451–1506), and other explorers after him, set foot on the New World, they were confronted with an unknown and mostly unexplainable territory. The gaps in the knowledge about this terra incognita were eagerly filled with handed-down, utopian fantasies of the Far East and the West. Columbus's first reports equated the New World with the Golden Age or the earthly paradise. Like the legendary land of milk and honey, it provides everything that is necessary for life. Food and mineral resources are plentiful, and a favorable climate enables several harvests a year. This paradise-like primordial condition resembles the Golden Age as imagined by the ancient poet Ovid in his *Metamorphoses*. The new continent was perceived as a "nourishing mother" – an "alma mater" – who selflessly and abundantly provides for her inhabitants.

At first sight, the Natives of the New World seem to fit seamlessly into this harmonious exchange with Mother Nature. However, many of these early travel reports do not render the Natives as solely positive. In these accounts, the "noble savages" often paradoxically distinguish

Figure 1.1 Woodcut from 1505, regarded as one of the earliest depictions of Native Americans.

Figure 1.2 "America," engraving by Theodor Galle (1571–1633) after a drawing by Jan van der Straet (Stradanus, 1523–1604).

themselves through gruesome cannibalistic practices. Countless early travel reports of the New World, together with their pictorial illustrations, follow this ambivalent logic.

The oldest known visual representation of American Indians, a woodcut from the early sixteenth century, shows this bipolar dimension. On one level, this representation features a female Native in the pose of a "nourishing mother," an image that must also be understood on an allegorical level. Like a mother who provides her child with everything it needs, the American continent will also provide in abundance for its inhabitants. Later allegories of America use similar visual strategies. An engraving from the early seventeenth century by Theodor Galle shows the discoverer Amerigo Vespucci next to a voluptuous female allegorization of America, idly reclining in a hammock and thus suggesting a land of plenty. In both visual portrayals, the depiction of America coincides with utopian, paradise-like fantasies.

However, upon closer examination, cannibals are lurking in the background, marring the idyllic nature of these visuals. In the woodcut with the depiction of American Indians, as well as in the later copper

4 *Discovery narratives*

engraving with Amerigo Vespucci, we see inhabitants who either consume humans or are preparing humans for consumption.

Exactly the same tension also governs the texts of early explorers, as, for example, **Amerigo Vespucci**'s (1452/54–1512) account of an incident during his third voyage in the early sixteenth century:

> The young man advanced and mingled among the women; they all stood around him, and touched and stroked him, wondering greatly at him. At this point a woman came down from the hill carrying a big club. When she reached the place where the young man was standing, she struck him such a heavy blow from behind

Figure 1.3 Woodcut depicting a scene from Amerigo Vespucci's voyages from the 1509 Strasbourg edition of his *Letter to Pier Soderini*.

that he immediately fell to the ground dead. The rest of the women at once seized him and dragged him by the feet up the mountain. ... There the women, who had killed the youth before our eyes, were now cutting him in pieces, showing us the pieces, roasting them at a large fire.

(138–139)

At first, a group of female Natives receives a young European sailor very positively, almost seductively, only to consequently kill, roast, and devour him before the eyes of the rest of the crew. Again, on the one hand, America is stylized as a benevolent female figure, guaranteeing abundance, but, on the other hand, she turns into a man-eating monster, lying in wait behind a caring façade.

The possibilities for explaining this paradox are many. It is obvious that these texts and visualizations operate with attraction and abjection as two seemingly opposing principles. We must not forget that these early texts and pictures mostly fulfilled an advertising function, inducing investors to finance further exploratory journeys and persuading potential settlers to enlist as colonists. In any case, the newly discovered land should be portrayed in the best way possible. What would work better than a utopian idealization of the land and its inhabitants? However, one could not portray the newly discovered territories as too perfect and ideal. After all, the colonial enterprise entailed – often under violent circumstances – the Europeans taking possession of the land. Cannibals were clearly better suited as the inevitable victims of colonial politics than strictly benevolent, noble savages of a Golden Age. The early picture of America therefore combines both traits: the utopian and the cannibalistic. Both dimensions mutually depend upon one another and make America prone to European colonial politics.

In the following centuries, the main elements of an earthly paradise as well as an uncontrollable wilderness remained connected with the different national identities in North and South America. Early knowledge of America in the European imagination in the late fifteenth and early sixteenth centuries hardly distinguished between regions. Reports from Central America, South America, or territories of what later became the United States merged in the consciousness of the reader into *one* relatively undifferentiated picture of the New World.

6 Discovery narratives

Thus, it is not surprising that this tension between paradise and wilderness has remained a leitmotif in the literature and the cultural history of the United States – even today.

Spaniards or seafarers traveling under the Spanish flag account for the earliest discoveries, as well as for forging a long-lasting image of the New World. The journeys of Columbus and Vespucci brought the Caribbean and South America to European awareness and inspired later conquistadors. With the conquest of the Aztec Empire (1519) in Mexico by Hernán Cortés, and the destruction of the Incan Empire in Peru (1533) by Francisco Pizarro, Spain forcibly secured its influence in Central and South America for centuries to come.

Spanish discoverers also visited the southern regions of the North American continent. **Álvar Núñez Cabeza de Vaca** (*c.*1490–*c.*1557) explored the area of today's Texas, New Mexico, and Arizona on foot from 1528 to 1536. As the only survivors of a group of three hundred men after a shipwreck in Florida, de Vaca and three companions marched from the outlet of the Mississippi River to Mexico City. The group endured unbelievable strains and deprivations, including several years as slaves in the hands of Native tribes. After eight years of hardship and several thousand miles on foot, they finally reached the Spanish settlement in Mexico City. De Vaca's report about his experiences was published in 1542 under the title *La Relación* and provides one of the earliest accounts of the southern territories of the United States. A few years after de Vaca, **Hernando de Soto** (1496 or 1500–1542) also explored the area of Florida and the Gulf Coast on a large-scale expedition with over six hundred soldiers. Driven by the futile search for gold and treasures, de Soto's four-year trip (1539–1542) was characterized by brutal interactions with local tribes, often resulting in atrocious killings of Natives.

Roughly speaking, at the same time as de Soto's venture into the Southeast, the Spanish crown commissioned a similar expedition to the Far West. Searching for the seven legendary golden cities of Cibola, **Francisco Vásques de Coronado** (1510–1554) set out in 1539 with an army of 350 soldiers, several hundred Natives, and a number of slaves. His journey led him from Mexico via Arizona, New Mexico, Texas, and Oklahoma into the area of today's Kansas. Splinter groups of his men even reached the Grand Canyon and came into contact with the pueblo tribes of the Hopi and Zuni. Needless to say, the search for the treasures of the legendary golden cities was not successful.

However, Spanish conquistadors and seafarers were not the only ones responsible for the discovery and exploration of the new continent. As early as 1497, only a few years after the first voyage of Columbus, the English king, Henry VII, sent the Italian **John Cabot** (*c.*1450–1498) on an exploratory journey into the Far North of America. Like Columbus half a decade before him, Cabot tried to reach Asia – this time by a supposedly shorter and more northern route. When he landed in Newfoundland, Labrador, and territories in New England, Cabot, like his predecessor, mistook them for China.

On a similar mission under French orders, the Italian **Giovanni da Verrazano** (1485–1528) in 1524 searched for a northwestern passage to Asia, thereby accidentally exploring the east coast of North America between Florida and Newfoundland. Sailing in the New York Bay as well as the lower reaches of the Hudson River, Verrazano believed he had found a passage to the Pacific. This misconception influenced cartography for a whole century, rendering America as a slim continent whose two landmasses form a narrow strait connecting the Atlantic with the Pacific.

The French continued to be instrumental in discovering and consequently colonizing the northern parts of the continent, including the territories of today's Canada. In 1534 **Jacques Cartier** (1491–1557) explored Newfoundland, traveled the St. Lawrence River, and gave Montreal its name. At the beginning of the seventeenth century, **Samuel de Champlain** (1567–1635) followed Cartier's footsteps. In 1608 he founded the city of Quebec as the capital of the colony of New France and discovered, among others, Lake Huron and Lake Champlain in Vermont. Samuel de Champlain's expeditions, taking him across the Atlantic over a dozen times, document in a unique way the life and customs of a number of Native tribes in North America. Champlain's close cooperation with the Huron tribe inevitably involved him and his men in conflicts between the Huron and the Iroquois. The countless publications of his experiences and observations are some of the most significant documents of North American conditions before or at the beginning of European colonial endeavors. His reports not only provide deep insights into the regions of today's

Canada, but also draw a detailed picture of the Native tribes in the northern coastal regions of today's United States before the advent of English colonists.

Champlain's reports highlight a fundamental difference in colonial politics between England and France. In the early phase of its overseas activities, France was mostly interested in the fur trade. By contrast, England tried to promote permanent settlements on an agricultural basis – as we will see with the example of Virginia. This inevitably entailed opposing relationship patterns in dealing with the Natives. While French fur traders relied on cooperation with the Natives as economical partners, the English settlers tended to enter into conflict with them over settlement areas.

Figure 1.4 Watercolor painting by John White depicting an Inuit man.

Even though England under Henry VII had participated in the first wave of explorations of the New World, England did not resume its American pursuits until the second half of the sixteenth century. Under Queen Elizabeth I, the search for a northwest passage continued. Between 1576 and 1578, the English seafarer **Martin Frobisher** (*c.*1535–1594) undertook several journeys into the northern parts of America. The realistic watercolor paintings by his companion **John White** (*c.*1540–1593) include the first pictures of the Inuit. Many of White's drawings of Native Americans functioned as models for book illustrations by the famous engraver Theodor de Bry (1528–1598), thus shaping the perception of North American Natives for centuries to come.

2 Colonial literature

A decisive change in English overseas policy took place in the latter part of the sixteenth century, when exploratory trips gave way to the first attempts at colonizing territories of today's United States. One of these ventures was **Sir Walter Raleigh**'s (*c*.1554–1618) Roanoke experiment in 1584. Legitimized through the Virginia Charter by Queen Elizabeth I, Raleigh attempted to establish a settlement on a small island off the coast of Virginia. Raleigh's companion, **Thomas Harriot** (*c*.1560–1621), supported this venture by a description of the land, which he later published under the title *Brief and True Report of the New-Found Land of Virginia* (1588). In a propaganda-like vein, Harriot's text expounds on the possibilities and riches of the colony in order to attract potential settlers. Harriot quotes long lists of raw materials and fruits in order to document the natural resources of the land. John White's watercolor paintings of the Natives and their customs served as models for the lavish illustrations of Harriot's text. The main goal of this book was to portray as temptingly as possible the abundance of wealth in the colony.

The frontispiece of Harriot's book, an illustration of the Garden of Eden, equates Virginia with an earthly paradise. Later on, Harriot compares the tattooed Native Americans of the region to the original population of ancient Britain. Harriot argues that America is now in a similar state as England was at the time of the Roman conquest more than 1,500 years ago. In ancient England, he writes, wild Picts decorated their bodies, thus resembling the practice of the Natives in this American colony. Since the age of colonization, Britain had developed from a land of tattooed savages into one of the most civilized and

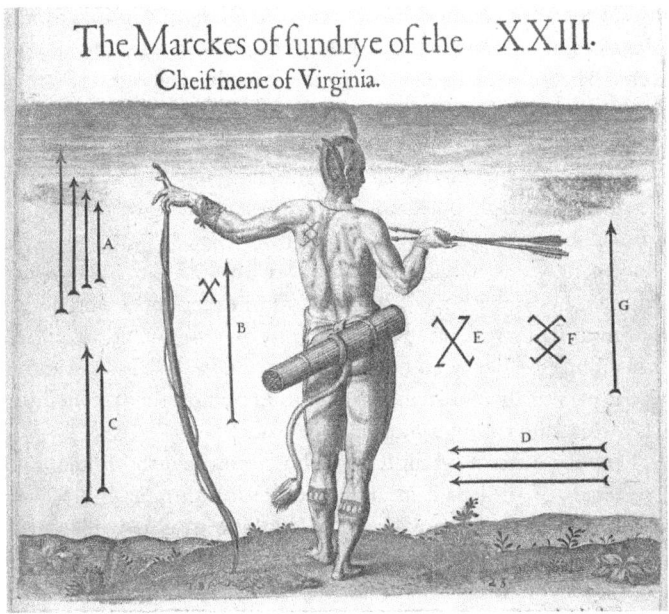

Figure 2.1 Engraving by Theodor de Bry, based on the work of John White, from Harriot's *Brief and True Report of the New-Found Land of Virginia* (1588) depicting a Native American.

mighty nations of the world. America – so Harriot concludes by analogy – will have a similarly successful future. Whoever invests now will clearly reap rich benefits.

Paradoxically, none of these expectations of the first British colony in America were fulfilled in the least. Roanoke went down in history as the Lost Colony. Bad leadership of the commanders, coupled with undiplomatic and even hostile contact with the Natives, made a permanent settlement difficult. The majority of the settlers had to be rescued by Sir Francis Drake. Two years later, no sign was found of the handful of men who were left behind to guard the settlement. In spite of these setbacks, Harriot's text went into print in 1588 and became one of the most influential early English reports about the New World.

After the disastrous result of the first colonization experiment in Roanoke, England reappears on the North American continent in the early seventeenth century. In this renewed attempt to gain a foothold in America, the Crown applied a novel business model. Instead of *one* selected person, who, like Sir Walter Raleigh, held all rights to a region in a "patent," the new company system favored larger groups of investors. King James I divided the coastal areas between Canada and Florida into two regions, transferring the rights to collaborating investment groups, which operated under the patronage of the so-called Virginia Company.

In this new phase, **Captain John Smith** (*c.*1580–1631) appeared on the stage of English colonial politics. His experiences were impressive: Smith had served in the Dutch army as a volunteer, later fought as a Habsburg soldier against the Turks, became a slave in the Ottoman Empire, eventually murdering his captor, escaping, and making his way back to England through Russia and Poland.

These experiences certainly contributed to the decision that Smith be selected to participate in an expedition to Virginia in 1607. His uncontrollable temper, however, got him into trouble while crossing the Atlantic. He was accused of mutiny and escaped his imminent execution in Virginia only because he was listed as one of the Council Members of the colony in a secret letter, which was to be opened after their arrival in Virginia. Such an important person had to be spared from execution. In fact, Smith was even elected governor of the colony. His imaginativeness and ability to negotiate with the Natives and receive food from the Indian tribes especially contributed to his political rise in the colony.

The colony of Jamestown, founded in 1607 on the James River in Virginia, became the first permanent English settlement in North America. During the first months of settling activities, John Smith led exploratory trips into the surrounding areas and got into armed conflicts with the Native tribes there. One of these conflicts, which supposedly left John Smith in the hands of the Indians, went down in American history as the Pocahontas myth.

John Smith reports in a short passage of his *General History of Virginia, New England, and the Summer Isles* (1624) how the Indians put him on trial and sentenced him to death:

> a long consultation was held, but the conclusion was, two great stones were brought before Powhatan [the chieftain]: then as many

as could laid hands on him [John Smith], dragged him to them, and thereon laid his head, and being ready with their clubs, to beat out his brains, Pocahontas the King's dearest daughter, when no entreaty could prevail, got his head in her arms, and laid her own upon his to save him from death.

(48)

This short episode, which is only mentioned in Smith's *General History*, has fueled the imagination of subsequent generations in many ways. Interestingly enough, what is at work here, once again, are the two opposing principles of the early image of America in the European imagination. On the one hand, the Natives embody violence and life-threatening danger; on the other hand, they ooze a benevolent, almost erotic, attraction. Both contradictory dimensions of the New World are paired in the Pocahontas story: imminent death and miraculous rescue, as well as atrocious repulsion and seductive attraction, seem to go hand in hand. Consequently, in the following centuries, Pocahontas became the epitome of the noble savage and *the* key allegory of colonial interaction between Europeans and Natives.

A few years earlier, the French writer **Michel de Montaigne** (1533–1592) had characterized the Natives of the New World in his essay "Des Cannibales" as noble savages, who lived in harmony with their surroundings. Pocahontas becomes a female version of this myth, in which eroticizing innocent femininity – an allegory of the New Continent – gets projected onto a concrete person. Just as Captain Smith faces danger cheek to cheek with the beautiful princess Pocahontas, so will generations of following adventurers imagine the interaction with the American frontier as an eroticizing thrill. It remains one of the unsolved mysteries of American colonial history whether these events are true to historical facts. Undeniable, however, is the influence this short passage of Smith's *General History* had on the subsequent image of America.

Captain John Smith not only had to face threats from Native Americans but also had to deal, again and again, with latent conflicts with the colonists in Jamestown. Once more, he was sentenced to death for the loss of two companions, escaped this sentence only by chance, and almost fell victim to a bomb attack. Against his will, Smith eventually had to retreat from the colony that he so decisively had helped to shape. Back in England, he wrote influential geographical works about the areas of New England and Virginia.

John Smith also offered his services to the Puritans who reached the coast of today's Massachusetts in 1620 on the *Mayflower*. Despite his excellent knowledge and his American experience, the Pilgrims rejected Smith's offer and preferred to trust his publications about America. His works seemed less problematic than his controversial personality.

In 1607 the so-called Separatists – Puritan groups who did not concur with the Church of England – left England and temporarily stayed in the Dutch city of Leyden. From the Netherlands, the Puritans tried to get permission to settle in Virginia, which they eventually received through a patent of the London Virginia Company. Under the leadership of **William Bradford** (1590–1657), about a hundred "Pilgrims" reached Plymouth in the area of today's Massachusetts. Due to bad weather conditions, the *Mayflower* landed north of the assigned area outside the jurisdiction of the Virginia Company. The legal uncertainty provided the settlers with some degree of independence from the Crown, which inspired the settlers to draft the so-called "Mayflower Compact" (1620). This kind of miniature constitution, which the Puritans called the "civil body politic," appears as the seed of self-organization and thus as the starting point of the American democratic self-image. The signatories united "for our better ordering and preservation . . . to . . . constitute . . . such just and equal Laws, Ordinances, Acts, Constitutions, and Offices . . . for the general good of the Colony" (76). Bradford established the "Mayflower Compact" in an extralegal area, or as he called it, "liberty," outside the jurisdiction of the Virginia Company, in which no one could exercise control over the Pilgrim Fathers "for none had power to command them" (75).

The best sources for the Plymouth Colony – which also contains the text of the "Mayflower Compact" – are the records of William Bradford in *Of Plymouth Plantation*. The texts document the fate of the Puritans during their stay in Leyden, the sea passage to America, and the development of the colony, thereby covering a time span from 1608 to 1647. Bradford's manuscript was thought to be lost for a long time, but surfaced again in the middle of the nineteenth century in the Bishop of London's library, being printed for the first time as late as 1856.

The fundamental orientation of American Puritanism, which is also reflected in Bradford's text, has substantially shaped the cultural-historical development of the United States. One of the most central tenets of American Puritanism is the principle of predestination or divine providence, developed from the writings of the Genevan reformer Johannes Calvin. According to this belief, God has predetermined whether a person will be saved or damned. Thus, the deeds of a person have no direct influence on his or her redemption since God has already predestined a person's fate. Differentiating between chosen and not-chosen people, this doctrine creates a very idiosyncratic sociopolitical dynamic.

Community members who did not fully subscribe to this belief were expelled from the congregation. **Roger Williams** (1603–1683), for example, was banned from Plymouth Colony because he supported a greater separation of church and state affairs within the colony. Through a number of pamphlets, Williams tried to propagate and disseminate his views. Quite remarkable is Williams's *A Key into the Language of America* (1643), supporting the protection of Natives in Providence, where he tried to establish a colony after his banishment. The book is also one of the oldest linguistic documents of Native American languages.

Williams's expulsion from the community resembles the fate of **Anne Hutchinson** (1591–1643), who was also banned from Plymouth Colony in the 1630s for nonconforming beliefs. Hutchinson, known for her intelligence and articulateness, was of the opinion that the inner workings of the Holy Spirit were solely responsible for the conversion of a person. Due to this attitude, she got into conflict with Puritan beliefs, which placed particular emphasis on the community for the conversion of people. A special synod dealt with her case, and when Hutchinson was not willing to renounce her own beliefs, she was excommunicated. While in exile, without protection from the community, she and her family were killed by Natives.

The involuntary exposure to American Indians was also the subject matter of **Mary Rowlandson**'s (*c*.1637–1711) book. Abducted by Native Americans, Rowlandson later published her experiences during her captivity in *A True History of the Captivity and Restoration of Mrs. Mary Rowlandson* (1682). Her story became the first bestseller in North America and served as a model for a plethora of frontier narratives stylizing Native Americans as an impending danger and cultural Other to European settlers.

A

NARRATIVE

OF THE

CAPTIVITY, SUFFERINGS AND REMOVES

OF

Mrs. *Mary Rowlandson*,

Who was taken Prisoner by the INDIANS with several others, and treated in the most barbarous and cruel Manner by those vile Savages : With many other remarkable Events during her TRAVELS.

Written by her own Hand, for her private Use, and now made public at the earnest Desire of some Friends, and for the Benefit of the afflicted.

BOSTON:

Printed and Sold at JOHN BOYLE's Printing-Office, next Door to the *Three Doves* in Marlborough-Street. 1773.

Figure 2.2 Title page of the 1773 edition of Mary Rowlandson's *A True History of the Captivity and Restoration of Mrs. Mary Rowlandson.*

Native Americans not only served as a physical threat in the discourses of the colonial period but also featured indirectly in shaping and defining Puritan identity. A prime example of how the Puritans defended their religious ideas and their way of life against people of different opinions by instrumentalizing the Natives is the clash with **Thomas Morton** (*c*.1579–1647). In 1625 Morton settled with a few of his people near the Puritan Plymouth. From Merry Mount – as Morton called his settlement – he soon entered into a business relationship with the Natives, supplying them with rum and weapons in exchange for furs. William Bradford called him a "lord of misrule," who operated a "school of Atheism" (205). When Morton had the nerve to erect a maypole in order to celebrate the departure of winter, the Puritans felt compelled to intervene. Accused of devoting himself to Bacchanalian rites, Morton was arrested and sent back to England. Despite these obstacles, Morton persisted in his ideas and returned to America a year later, but his weapons dealings with the Natives once again served as an excuse for arresting him. This time, the Puritans even burned down his property to prevent him from resuming his activities.

From his exile in England, Morton tried in vain to convince influential people that the Puritans in New England had assumed too much power and therefore were betraying the Anglican Church and the Crown. In 1637 he published his justification against the Puritans under the title *New English Canaan*. Morton's text represents an important non-Puritan perspective and an opposing point of view on early New England history. As late as 1836, this conflict with Puritan authorities inspired Nathaniel Hawthorne to write his short story "The May-Pole of Merry Mount." By using this historical case study of Puritan self-righteousness, Hawthorne critically deals with the Puritan legacy that was still at work in nineteenth-century America.

A key element of Puritan self-understanding is the Calvinistic principle of predestination, which culminates in the belief of the early colonists that their American settlement is God's chosen colony. Until today, this notion of a nation chosen by God dominates the self-image of the United States and is still used to legitimize steps in foreign policy. However, despite these repressive tendencies, which lead to the exclusion of people with differing views, American Puritanism, with its special kind of church organization, can also be seen as a nucleus of

American democratic understanding. The self-organization of independent congregations, joining each other in a local church with a written covenant and with a minister, reflects a deeply rooted democratic inclination.

At the beginning of the twentieth century, the German sociologist Max Weber provided a stringent, but nonetheless controversial, explanation of the role of Puritanism and Protestant religion, respectively, on the socioeconomic development of the United States. In his groundbreaking paper "The Protestant Ethic and the Spirit of Capitalism" (1904), Weber ties the Lutheran view of the God-given talent and purpose of an individual to the Calvinist concept of predestination. For Protestants, to be chosen as a human being manifests itself in material success. Therefore, an inherent pursuit of financial wealth drives Protestant countries like the United States. According to Max Weber, this orientation toward individual success, legitimized by the concept of predestination, creates a capitalist tendency in countries with a high proportion of Protestant inhabitants.

Puritan writing in America becomes the prime example of the forces that Weber singles out as typical for this Protestant work ethic. A decade after the Pilgrims landed at Plymouth Rock, approximately seven hundred religiously motivated settlers founded the Massachusetts Bay Colony in 1630. While crossing the Atlantic, **John Winthrop** (1588–1649), who later became governor of the colony, charted the ideals for the future colony in his sermon-like pamphlet *A Model for Christian Charity*. This colony was intended to be a paradigm of a harmonious and exemplary Christian community. "For we must consider that we shall be as a City upon a Hill, the eyes of all people are upon us" (10). Here, Winthrop draws on a famous quote from the Gospel according to Matthew (Matt. 5:14), in which believers are likened to a city upon a hill. By using this analogy, Winthrop bestows upon the settlement a biblical dimension of predestination and an exemplary function for the rest of the world. Winthrop's *A Model for Christian Charity* is an early instance of the sermon-like homiletic prose that will dominate the literary output of Colonial America over the next century.

Sermons, diaries, and journals of influential colonists are among the most important specimens of literary production in New England. A good example of this genre is *The Journal of John Winthrop* (1790,

1825, 1826), which documents and comments on the development of the young colony in diary-like entries, including passages on dissenters such as Roger Williams and Anne Hutchinson.

The three generations of the Mather family in New England were important literary proponents of these text types and the Puritan idea in general. **Richard Mather** (1596–1669) emigrated from England to America in 1635 after having been removed from his position as priest by the Anglican Church for his unconventional religious views. He became the most influential priest of the newly founded Massachusetts Bay Colony and is considered to be one of the founding fathers of the settlement. His *Journal* documents numerous details about his life before the backdrop of the evolving colony. While the journal of Richard Mather was not published until 1850, his translation of the psalms in the *Bay Psalm Book* (1640) was the first book to be printed on New England soil. Richard Mather was also engaged in a heated internal Church dispute on whether only the children of full members of the parish were allowed to receive baptism. This highly controversial issue not only drove a wedge between members of the colony but also divided Richard Mather and his son Increase.

Increase Mather (1639–1723), who studied at Harvard College and in Europe, also worked as a preacher in England during the Puritan interregnum (1649–1660). With the restoration of the monarchy, he had to leave England and return to America. In Massachusetts, he became president of Harvard College and commented on the political aspects of the colony in a series of writings. Whether in these political texts or in his writings on natural science, the praise for divine creation always stands in the foreground. This logic becomes especially apparent in his tracts on comets but also in his treatises on the war with the Natives, which he interprets as an allegory of a fight between the Natives, as the forces of evil, and the white settlers, as the representatives of good.

With **Cotton Mather** (1663–1728), the son of Increase Mather and thus the grandson of Richard Mather, this dualistic worldview enters the third generation. In *The Wonders of the Invisible World* (1693), Cotton Mather continues the self-indulgent Puritan sense of mission when he writes: "The New-Englanders are a People of God settled in those, which were once the Devil's Territories" (13). In his main work *Magnalia Christi Americana* (1702), a history of New England, he refers to the deeds of the settlers as a war of the Lord against the Natives and those of other faiths. Cotton Mather also writes extensively on the so-called Salem witchcraft trials – one of the darkest episodes in the early history of New England. After accusing numerous people of witchcraft, the judges in these trials eventually sentenced fourteen women and five men to death by hanging.

Cotton Mather was not actively involved in the trials nor did he firmly speak out against the convictions. Cotton's father Increase, on the other hand, took a critical stand against the witchcraft trials, questioning verdicts with the help of so-called "spectral evidence." The belief that a person appeared as a ghost ("specter") to someone in a dream or a vision could be used as evidence of their witchery. Cotton Mather describes this phenomenon by using the example of Martha Carrier, who supposedly performed horrible witchcraft on other people in their dreams: "Martha Carrier, or her Shape, that grievously tormented them, by Biting, Pricking, Pinching or Choaking of them" (154).

A few years after the verdicts and executions, these witch hunts were generally considered to have been wrong. Nevertheless, the Salem witchcraft trials have continued to be embedded in the collective memory of the United States in general and American literature in particular. Arthur Miller's famous play *The Crucible* (1953), for example, compares the witch hunt of the late seventeenth century to the prosecution of alleged communists by Senator Joseph McCarthy in the Cold War period. Also, the terrorist scare after 9/11, which turned dissenters into potential enemies of the state, conjured up analogies to this Puritan witch hunt.

However, the Puritan context of the colonies in the sixteenth and seventeenth centuries did not just generate sermons and religiously motivated theological prose. The first literary figure on the North American continent to produce literary texts outside of these narrowly confined religious formats was **Anne Bradstreet** (*c*.1612–1672). As the wife of the later governor of the Massachusetts Bay Colony and mother of eight children, Anne Bradstreet processed her experiences in her poems. Because of her good education, which she received as the daughter of a wealthy steward to an earl in aristocratic England, Bradstreet was able to combine the Elizabethan lyrical forms of Spenser and Sidney with her colonial experiences. Without her knowledge,

Anne Bradstreet's brother-in-law took her poems with him to England and published them under the title *The Tenth Muse Lately Sprung up in America* in 1650. This collection is considered to be the first printed publication of poems written on American soil.

Bradstreet's poems give insight into the psyche and daily life of a woman and mother in a colonial society, marked by extreme sacrifice. Her texts document the inner debates over personal tragedies like fire disasters or the death of children and grandchildren. Bradstreet reflects on this very personal female perspective of her texts in the prologue to her collection of poetry by subliminally positioning her *oeuvre* in a coded protofeminist manner:

> To sing of War, of Captains, and of Kings,
> Of Cities founded, Common-wealths begun,
> For my mean pen are too superiour things.
>
> (1–3)

Bradstreet does not take on the cosmic voice of a bard singing about the founding of a nation – as does, for example, Vergil in the *Aeneid*, to which these verses probably allude. On the contrary, she deliberately devotes herself to the microcosm of colonial everyday life from a woman's point of view. Many of Bradstreet's poems start with a real event, such as the fire that burned her family's home to the ground. In the poem, "Verses upon the Burning of Our House, July 10th, 1666," Bradstreet first describes the sorrow and the material loss that the fire caused:

> Here stood that Trunk, and there that chest;
> There lay that store I counted best.
> My pleasant things in ashes lye.
>
> (25–27)

Then the poem takes an unexpected turn. Suddenly, she leaves behind the material world of the colony and reads the loss of her house with respect to the immaterial home that God in his kindness has prepared for her in the eternity of heaven:

> Thou hast an house on high erect,
> Fram'd by that mighty Architect,

> With glory richly furnished,
> Stands permanent tho: this bee fled.
>
> (43–46)

This inner dialogue between personal reality and religious interpretation is characteristic of Bradstreet's poetry, integrating itself seamlessly into the Puritan belief in a divinely predestined world.

What is remarkable, however, is that Bradstreet's trial-like monologues with God do not always fully eliminate the implied criticism of God's deeds. When she was grieving over the death of her granddaughter, in the poem "In Memory of My Dear Grandchild Elizabeth Bradstreet, Who Deceased August, 1665, Being a Year and a Half Old," the accusations against God do not seem to be resolvable with religious rationalizations:

> By nature Trees do rot when they are grown.
> And Plums and Apples throughly ripe do fall,
> And Corn and grass are in their season mown,
> And time brings down what is both strong and tall.
> But plants new set to be eradicate,
> And buds new blown, to have so short a date,
> Is by his hand alone that guides nature and fate.
>
> (8–14)

For many lines, Anne Bradstreet accusingly compares the death of the child with unnatural occurrences in nature. Only the last line superficially accepts these events as God's decisions. However, the accusation against the creator of this situation remains as a silent rebellion against God's will.

Aside from Anne Bradstreet, **Edward Taylor** (*c.*1644–1729) stands out as a poet in the early colonial period. Taylor also uses contemporary role models, like the Metaphysical poets, and adapts their style for his specific religious concerns. For example, in his poem "Huswifery," he uses "conceits," a popular stylistic feature in metaphysical poetry in England during the seventeenth century. Conceits are far-fetched metaphors, linking two very different concepts:

> Make me, O Lord, thy Spin[n]ing Wheele compleat;
> Thy Holy Worde my Distaff make for mee.

Make mine Affections thy Swift Flyers neate,
And make my Soule thy holy Spoole to bee.
My Conversation make to be thy Reele,
And reele the yarn thereon spun of thy Wheele.

(1–6)

In this concrete example, Taylor equates the lyrical "I" with different objects and the imagery of cloth production. The speaker considers himself to be a tool for God's will, just as the spinning wheel and spool are tools for making cloth.

It is noteworthy that Taylor's work was not published until the 1930s. His complete works lay undiscovered as manuscripts in the Yale Library for centuries. Among these hidden treasures were his so-called *Preparatory Meditations* – poems concerning certain biblical passages. Taylor, being a minister of the frontier-town of Westfield, probably used them in order to prepare for and immerse himself in his sermons. The discovery of the manuscripts in the first half of the twentieth century shed a completely new light on the literary landscape of New England's Puritan era. Most surprising was the fact that a Puritan minister could be so profoundly interested in poetry.

As mentioned before, the primary genre of Puritan literary self-expression continued to be the sermon, which, during the middle of the eighteenth century, the Puritan clergy in New England prolifically employed to propagate a radical religious renewal called the "Great Awakening." One of these charismatic preachers was **Jonathan Edwards** (1703–1758), who in the 1730s gathered several hundred believers in a short amount of time in North Hampton, sending them into religious raptures.

As in Puritan poetry, Edwards uses conceits in his sermons, supporting religious content with concrete metaphors, the most famous example being the sermon "Sinners in the Hands of an Angry God" (1741). Here, Edwards compares humans to a spider being held over the fire by God, who decides whether a person is saved or damned:

The God that holds you over the pit of hell, much as one holds a spider, or some loathsome insect over the fire, abhors you, and is dreadfully provoked: his wrath towards you burns like fire; he looks upon you as worthy of nothing else, but to be cast into the fire; he is of purer eyes than to bear to have you in his sight; you are ten thousand times more abominable in his eyes, than the most hateful venomous serpent is in ours.

(159)

The Awakening movement combines traditional Calvinist concepts of predestination, like man in the hand of God, with ideas of Enlightenment philosophy. In his "Personal Narrative" (1765), Edwards, for example, recalls his religious awakening as an adolescent in a diction very much reminiscent of John Locke's *An Essay Concerning Human Understanding* (1690):

I walked abroad alone, in a solitary place in my father's pasture, for contemplation. And as I was . . . looking up on the sky and clouds, there came into my mind so sweet a sense of the glorious majesty and grace of God. . . . I seemed to see them both in a sweet conjunction; majesty and meekness joined together. . . . After this my sense of divine things gradually increased . . . and had more of that inward sweetness. The appearance of every thing was altered; there seemed to be, as it were, a calm, sweet cast, or appearance of divine glory, in almost every thing.

(84–85)

Here, sensory impressions are closely linked with religious insight; meditative contemplation changes the seemingly objective sensory world. By internalizing the appearance of things, Edwards perceives these things as expressions of a praise of God. In fact, the majority of Edwards's texts deal with aspects of meditative belief, manifesting itself in a mystic state of emotion.

The strong religious influence still at work in New England's literature of the second half of the eighteenth century is also visible in the works of **Phillis Wheatley** (1753–1784), the earliest African-American poet. Phillis, born in the early 1750s in West Africa, came to America on a slave ship. At the age of eight, she was bought by the Wheatley family from Boston as a household slave. The liberal Wheatleys noticed the girl's talent and supplied her with an above-average schooling, surpassing even the standards for a white girl's education at the time.

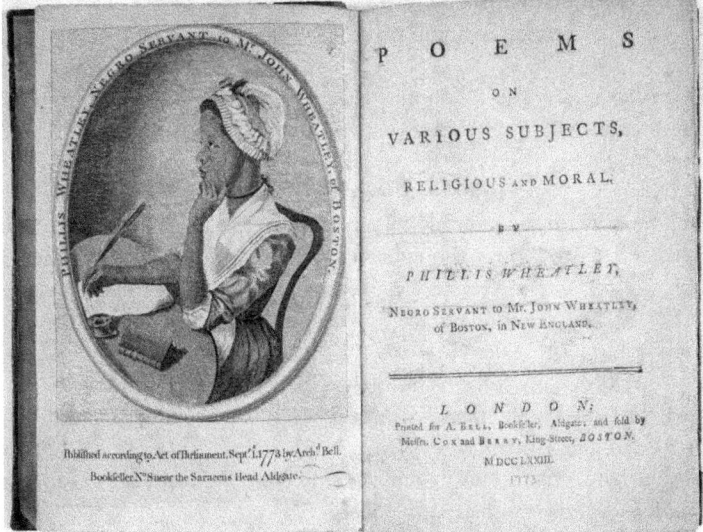

Figure 2.3 Title page of Phillis Wheatley's *Poems on Various Subjects* (1773).

In 1773 Wheatley's *Poems on Various Subjects* appeared, being the first publication by an African-American author. She entered the literary circles of the time, but her talent was grotesquely showcased as something exotic and sensational. For the publication of her volume of poetry, for example, a commission ensured that Phillis Wheatley was indeed the author.

A very prominent motif in Wheatley's texts is her African origin. Her poem "On Being Brought from Africa to America" (1773) discusses the ambivalence of her own identity between pagan roots and a Christian philosophy of salvation:

'Twas mercy brought me from my Pagan land,
Taught my benighted soul to understand
That there's a God, that there's a Saviour too:
Once I redemption neither sought nor knew.
Some view our sable race with scornful eye,
"Their colour is a diabolic die."

> Remember, Christians, Negroes, black as Cain,
> May be refin'd, and join th'angelic train.

Wheatley clearly uses a "double-voiced" discourse, a typical feature of the literature of oppressed groups in general. On the one hand, she uses the dominating language of the oppressor ("'Twas mercy brought me from my Pagan land"); on the other hand, however, she questions this very discourse by stating: "Remember, Christians, Negroes, black as Cain, may . . . join the angelic train." The Christian doctrine of salvation was bestowed on her through her enslavement. However, this very same doctrine of salvation is in utter contrast to the Christian racist attitudes that deny human equality to blacks.

After the death of the Wheatleys, Phillis was freed according to her owner's last will. She married a free African American who, unfortunately, struggled financially, endangering their very existence. Even though she continuously published poetry, Wheatley died during childbirth, impoverished at the age of 31.

Besides religious literature, the genre of travel reports remained very popular from the Age of Discovery into the eighteenth century. A late example of such a narrative is the records of **Sarah Kemble Knight** (1666–1727). In her private diary, she documents a journey from Boston to New York in 1704–1705, providing a critical insight into the lives of settlers in the rural areas of the Northeast. The reader experiences the unfiltered perspective of an educated woman from Boston on what she considered to be the coarse backwoods colonialists outside the urban centers of New England.

Another notable writer is **William Byrd** (1674–1744) with his report about the survey of the border between Virginia and North Carolina in 1728–1729, reflecting on the perceived contrasts between the southern aristocracy and common people. With their implied bias and realism, these eyewitness accounts from the eighteenth century contrast with the often utopian nature of earlier travel reports written during the Age of Discovery.

3 Literature of the Early Republic

Following the European tradition of idealizing America as the promised land, the Frenchman **J. Hector St. John de Crèvecoeur** (1735–1813) produced his *Letters from an American Farmer* (1782) – one of the most influential treatises of the transition period from Colonies to Early Republic. Crèvecoeur considers America an idealized alternative to the European forms of monarchy and aristocracy, praising American agriculture as an exemplary model for a nation rooted in equality:

> Here are no aristocratical families, no courts, no kings, no bishops, no ecclesiastical dominion, no invisible power giving to a few a very visible one; no great manufacturers employing thousands, no great refinements of luxury. The rich and the poor are not so far removed from each other as they are in Europe. ... We are a people of cultivators ... united by the silken bands of mild government, all respecting the laws, without dreading their power, because they are equitable.
>
> (35–36)

Crèvecoeur links antiaristocratic and antimonarchic views with major political questions of the time, all of which revolve around the visions and achievements of the American and French revolutions. Crèvecoeur's writings had a tremendous influence, both on the European image of America as well as on America's self conception in the nineteenth century. Creating a retrogressive utopian America, based on a preindustrial agrarian ideal is, however, rather untypical for American self-fashioning. America, from its early days on, has hardly ever perceived its ideal state as a retrospective myth, but has rather tended to mythologize the future as a locus for self-realization instead.

In his pamphlet *Common Sense* (1776), **Thomas Paine** (1737–1809) pursues the same line of democratic propaganda on a philosophical and programmatic level. In this extremely popular text, Paine adapts Locke's notion of the freedom of the individual for an American ideology of Enlightenment, which simultaneously propagates autonomy from the colonial power of England.

The multifaceted striving for American independence culminates in 1776 in the Declaration of Independence and ends after the revolutionary wars when England finally acknowledges the independence of the United States in 1783. Intellectually, the separation process manifests itself in a variety of ways. The linguist **Noah Webster** (1758–1843), for example, is one of the first to define American identity on a linguistic level. In his *Dissertation on the English Language* (1789), he advocates American English as an idiom that has emancipated itself from British dominance. Together with his *American Dictionary of the English Language* (1828), Webster formed the linguistic basis of American English, thereby propagating, for the newly emerging United States, an idiosyncratic medium of self-expression that is distinct from the former oppressor's language.

However, the person who best embodies the transition from the Puritan religiosity of the American colonies to the enlightened independence of the Early Republic is **Benjamin Franklin** (1706–1790). With only two years of formal school education, the autodidact and apprentice printer from Philadelphia eventually became an important newspaper editor. In his official function as postmaster general he was also to oversee the dissemination of his own products, thereby securing a wide audience for his print media. Despite being mostly self-taught, Franklin gained international fame and recognition as a scientist beyond the United States for his research on electricity and the invention of the lightning rod.

Throughout his life, even as a young man, Franklin displayed a strong sense of political awareness and civic responsibility, founding public libraries, volunteer fire brigades, and other institutions of common interest. At the age of 42, he withdrew from operational business life to devote himself to political activities, which culminated in his role as one of the Founding Fathers of the United States.

In addition to Franklin's diverse scientific and political achievements, his multifaceted personality also shows in his writing career. Even in his early years, he successfully published *Poor Richard's Almanack* (1732–1758), a yearbook of popular worldly wisdom and aphorisms. It anticipates central elements of his later *Autobiography*, which he wrote, with interruptions, from 1771 onward until his death in 1790. The *Autobiography* offers its readers insights into the psyche and the worldview of a major public figure of eighteenth-century America. It shows Franklin's conflicting character traits: on the one hand, it displays the deeply rooted religious traditions of colonial America, and, on the other, the desire to embrace the secular ideas of the Enlightenment, prevailing in the second half of the eighteenth century.

Extensive passages of Franklin's *Autobiography,* therefore, read like textbook examples of a Protestant work ethic, as advocated by Max Weber at the beginning of the twentieth century. Until today, Franklin's self-portrayal has remained a classic instance of Puritan self-realization and self-analysis, typical for the successful "homo Americanus." Particularly telling are the passages in which Franklin lists thirteen virtues (temperance, silence, order, etc.) for each day of the week in a specifically devised grid that allowed him to mark his shortcomings with a black dot, keeping accounts of his life, similar to a bookkeeper. Other examples are his to-do lists, regulating his daily routines into strict time windows for specific tasks, reminiscent of the balance sheets of an accountant. For generations Franklin's combination of introspection and self-regulation became a role model for what Americans should strive for in order to become good citizens, and, at the same time, excel economically. Until today Franklin's *Autobiography* has held the status of a "how-to" manual for achieving the American dream of the "self-made man."

Notions of Protestant self-education and ideas of the Enlightenment visibly contributed to Franklin's role in the American Revolution. For example, he left his mark on the *Declaration of Independence* (1776), the most important text of the emerging United States of America. Drafted by **Thomas Jefferson** (1743–1826), Franklin's revisions clearly show signs of Franklin's own heritage and the *Zeitgeist* of the period. For instance, in the sentence "We hold these truths to be sacred and undeniable," Franklin replaced "sacred and undeniable" with "self-evident" (Jefferson 36). It seems as if he wanted to distance

FORM OF THE PAGES.

TEMPERANCE.
Eat not to dulness: drink not to elevation.

	Sun.	M.	T.	W.	Th.	F.	S.
Tem.							
Sil.	*	*		*		*	
Ord.	*	*	*		*	*	*
Res.		*				*	
Fru.		*				*	
Ind.			*				
Sinc.							
Jus.							
Mod.							
Clea.							
Tran.							
Chas.							
Hum.							

Figure 3.1 List of thirteen virtues for each day of the week from *The Autobiography of Benjamin Franklin* (1771–1790).

himself from the Puritan religious past, turning toward the new era of Enlightenment, where religion gives way to reason. Franklin's Janus-like persona thus perfectly embodies the age of transition from Revolution to Early Republic, a period that he so decisively helped to shape. Despite his diverse achievements, Franklin's greatest literary contribution is his *Autobiography*, which placed the cornerstone for a popular genre of fiction in the nineteenth and twentieth centuries.

The Early Republic tried to adapt the genre of the novel to the American situation in a variety of ways. Modern novels developed as a new text type in England during the eighteenth century, due to a unique combination of sociocultural factors, such as a wealthy middle

Literature of the Early Republic 31

Figure 3.2 Neoclassical villa of Monticello, designed by Thomas Jefferson, photograph by Moritz Klarer.

class whose purchasing power was coupled with a high literacy rate, low printing costs in combination with a royalty system for authors, as well as effective distribution channels for selling and disseminating the texts. In the United States, the novel only emerged toward the end of the eighteenth century, mostly adopting or adapting topics that also dominated the British novel.

One of the most important subgenres was the "sentimental novel," appealing to the "sentiment," that is, the compassion of the reader. It mostly portrays the fates of women, showing them in precarious situations created by male, often sexual, violence. British examples are Samuel Richardson's (1689–1761) highly successful novels *Pamela: Or, Virtue Rewarded* (1740) and *Clarissa: Or, the History of a Young Lady* (1748), both dealing with the harassment of a young girl. The most important American example of this genre is **William Hill Brown**'s (1765–1793) *The Power of Sympathy* (1789). It tells the tragic stories of four women, most of which end in suicide. Also **Hannah Foster**'s (1758–1840) sentimental epistolary novel *The Coquette; or,*

The History of Eliza Wharton (1797) revolves around sexual seduction, resulting in unwanted pregnancy and finally the death of the female protagonist.

One might wonder why these empathetic plots gained such wide popularity, and why readers seemed to be so interested in the suffering of others. The English philosopher Edmund Burke had asked the same questions already in the middle of the eighteenth century. According to his view, the distress of others creates a voyeuristic interest in the beholder, together with an almost paradoxical pleasure that derives from watching. Seeing others suffer raises the onlooker's awareness, and, according to Burke, is likely to prompt action in order to do something against the victim's agony. In short, the apparently innate voyeuristic pleasure, deriving from watching others suffer, has a humanitarian benefit after all. Whether Burke's explanation is correct or not, is not the major issue here. What is important is that, indirectly, it legitimized the sentimental novel through didactic and humanitarian values. This is noteworthy since, prior to the sentimental tradition, novels were thought to be dangerous for fostering moral corruption, particularly in female readers.

This alleged danger, emanating from reading fiction, is at the heart of picaresque novels, which had a long tradition in Europe with works such as Miguel de Cervantes's *Don Quijote* (1605, 1615). Following British examples, the American author **Tabitha Tenney** (1762–1837) wrote her *Female Quixotism* (1801), an adventurous-satirical novel about a heroine who loses her grip on reality due to excessive reading. The protagonist tries to apply literary standards to the real world, creating unrealistically high expectations for finding a partner. Ultimately, she ends up alone, suffering the ridicule of the people around her.

Alongside the sentimental and the picaresque novels, the Early Republic also adopted the highly popular European genre of the Gothic novel. These uncanny and spooky novels, which go back to Horace Walpole's (1717–1797) *The Castle of Otranto* (1764), are usually set in medieval European castles. This presented very special challenges for American authors since the typical European settings of the English Gothic novel were not available in the United States. The American author **Charles Brockden Brown** (1771–1810) reflected on this particular problem in the preface to his novel *Edgar Huntly, Or, Memoirs of a Sleepwalker* (1799). For the American Gothic novel Brown deems "incidents of Indian hostility, and the perils of the Western wilderness . . . far more suitable" (4) than "Gothic castles and chimeras" (4). As indicated in the preface, Edgar Huntly, the main character of the novel, has to endure situations of the classic Gothic novel in the aforementioned American settings and contexts. This includes being attacked by Native Americans or being trapped in the dark of a labyrinth-like cave for several days.

During Edgar Huntly's attempt to solve the murder of a friend, he encounters the sleepwalking servant Clithero on a farm near Philadelphia. Edgar suspects him to be the culprit, especially since Clithero confesses to Edgar a complicated story from his past in Ireland, also involving the death of a person. Awakening one night, Edgar does not find himself in his own bed but in a completely dark room, which turns out to be part of a maze-like cave. Near death, due to dehydration and exhaustion, he is attacked by a panther. Edgar manages to kill the animal, drink its blood, and thereby save himself from dying of thirst. As Edgar finally finds a way out of the cave, he kills a group of Native Americans in order to save a captured white girl they are holding hostage. At the end of the novel, Edgar realizes that he, like Clithero, is a somnambulist, which also explains how he ended up in the cave without his knowledge. In addition to that, Huntly finds out that Clithero, whom he suspected to have murdered his friend, is innocent because his friend either died during a Native American attack or committed suicide.

Although the plot might seem chaotic, and at times utterly unrealistic, Brown's novel *Edgar Huntly* stands out from early American fiction for two major reasons: Brown adapted the English Gothic novel for American settings, and, probably even more importantly, he introduced unusual psychological dimensions to the genre. Especially in the passages in which the desperate main character tries to escape the labyrinth of the cave, Brown anticipates elements of the dark and abject aesthetic of Edgar Allan Poe. Brown also explores near-death and extreme situations and dwells on the abnormal and the psychologically exceptional. Despite these innovative qualities, or maybe precisely because of them, Brown was one of the first American novelists to be able to make a living from his writing, and, at the same time, receive critical attention in Europe.

One of the first American authors of the Early Republic to gain full international recognition was **Washington Irving** (1783–1859). Already in his youth, Irving wrote letters for his brother's newspaper, publishing under the pseudonym of Jonathan Oldstyle. Numerous journeys to Europe with multiyear stays brought Irving into contact with important scientists and artists of his time, contacts that inspired and furthered his career as a writer. Irving's *A History of New York* (1809), allegedly written by the imaginary Diedrich Knickerbocker, was an immediate success. The book is a burlesque and satirical parody of New York's history in which Irving recounts incidents from the days of the discoverers to the Dutch colonists, ending with the acquisition of New York by the English in 1664. Despite its historical setting, the book parodies important contemporary figures like Thomas Jefferson. Beyond this kind of historiographical parody, Irving also very successfully dealt with historical topics in his *oeuvre*. *The Life and Voyages of Christopher Columbus* (1828) remained the most important biography of the explorer until the end of the nineteenth century.

During a seventeen-year stay in Europe where Irving did business for the family company, he also came into contact with important authors such as Sir Walter Scott and Samuel Taylor Coleridge. *The Sketch Book of Geoffrey Crayon, Gent.* (1819–1820), which was a great success both in England and the United States, was a product of this time period. The collection, which includes his most famous tales "Rip van Winkle" and "The Legend of Sleepy Hollow," marks the beginning of the long and influential tradition of the American short story. Some of its individual stories have held a myth-like quality in the American collective memory for almost two centuries.

"Rip van Winkle" is a story about a henpecked scallywag in a small town on the Hudson River. Set before the American War of Independence, it indirectly allegorizes the beginning of an independent American narrative tradition. During a hunting excursion in the Catskill Mountains, Rip van Winkle meets the ghosts of the old Dutch founding fathers of the Hudson River region and afterward falls into a twenty-year sleep. Upon his return to the village, everything has changed. His oppressive wife is dead and the North American colonies have gained their independence. The sign above the village inn no longer shows King George but George Washington instead, although, upon closer inspection, the "old George" still shines through:

> He recognized on the sign, however, the ruby face of King George, under which he had smoked so many a peaceful pipe; but even this was singularly metamorphosed. The red coat was changed for one of blue and buff, a sword was held in the hand instead of a sceptre, the head was decorated with a cocked hat, and underneath was printed in large characters, GENERAL WASHINGTON.
>
> (237)

Rip van Winkle thus becomes, similar to Irving himself, a character of transition and of a new beginning. On the one hand, both are still rooted in the traditions of the colonies, depending on European authorities, such as the Dutch or the English, but on the other hand, a new self-confidence literally awakens in them. Being the first major American short story, Irving's "Rip van Winkle" renders the new beginning of American literature also on a metafictional level by making its protagonist, Rip van Winkle, embody this very notion of transformation and reorientation.

Another American author, whose fiction attained international fame and was immediately translated into a number of languages, was **James Fenimore Cooper** (1789–1851). Using Sir Walter Scott as his model, Cooper produced the first historical novels in American literature. Arranged around the romanticized relationship between the white Natty Bumppo and his Mohican "brother" Chingachgook, Cooper's *Leatherstocking Tales* (1823–1841) anticipate numerous later narratives and films, negotiating the American frontier with its tensions between Europeans and Natives. The most famous of the five *Leatherstocking* novels is Cooper's *The Last of the Mohicans* (1826), which, despite being an example of the historical novel, also contains major features of romanticism. Especially the character of Natty, who, although being the son of white parents, grew up among Natives, functions as a cultural hybrid and negotiator between European and Native cultures. Natty's own behavior incorporates stereotypically Indian features, as, for example, his proto-ecological respect for the forest and his hunting habits that allow him only to kill as much as he needs to survive. By romanticizing a nature-oriented lifestyle oriented to nature and by modeling this philosophy to a large extent on Native American culture as an expression of nature, Cooper unintentionally anticipates the major tenets of transcendentalism.

4 Transcendentalism

Arising in the first half of the nineteenth century, transcendentalism was the first, and maybe the most important, indigenous American intellectual movement. Despite its strong literary inclination, it was not confined to literature but also branched out into religious, philosophical, and sociopolitical areas. Transcendentalism is causally connected to the writer and philosopher **Ralph Waldo Emerson** (1803–1882). After the death of his wife, the Harvard graduate and priest experienced an existential crisis with profound religious doubts, forcing him to abandon the priesthood. During a stay in Europe, he met, among others, the poets Samuel Taylor Coleridge and William Wordsworth, both "founders" of English romanticism, a movement that was to influence and shape transcendentalism in a decisive way. Returning to the States, Emerson became a popular lecturer whose performances still showed traces of his former religious office but tended to probe larger philosophical questions. From the mid-1830s on, he belonged to a circle of intellectuals known as the transcendentalists, including Nathaniel Hawthorne, Henry David Thoreau, Margaret Fuller, and Amos Bronson Alcott.

Emerson's first book, the essay-like *Nature* (1836), already contained all of the important principles of the transcendentalist movement, especially a critique of the traditionalist bias of education and learning at the time. Dealing with the "dry bones of the past" (7), according to Emerson, seemed more important to his contemporaries than directly dealing with the things in front of them: "Our age is retrospective. It builds on the sepulchers of our fathers" (7). In order to escape from this orientation toward the past, Emerson propagates an inexperienced and fresh view on the world, leaving behind the burden of tradition. His subsequent essays, "Self-Reliance" (1841) and "The American Scholar" (1837), further expand and advocate the notion of a direct, individual access to the world, or, as he calls it, nature. This new start also changed the way in which conveyed knowledge was to be received. Emerson, for example, pleaded for an individual and unobstructed access to literature: "There is then creative reading as well as creative writing" (59). His programmatically questioning any kind of tradition in all areas of life naturally also affected American literature, which, at the time, was trying to break the shackles of European models.

Despite its originality, Emerson's philosophy shows important influences of European romanticism, such as the direct relationship of the individual with nature and the associated belief that nature can serve as a starting point for transcendental self-awareness. The urge to blend in with nature becomes most evident in the famous "transparent eyeball" passage from Emerson's *Nature*:

> Standing on the bare ground, – my head bathed by the blithe air, and uplifted into infinite space, – all mean egotism vanishes. I become a transparent eye-ball; I am nothing; I see all; the currents of the Universal Being circulate through me; I am part or particle of God.
>
> (10)

Emerson sees the individual as mystically united with the world. The individual thus becomes an invisible, perceptive eye that is observing nature, and, at the same time, is also part of nature.

In order to achieve such closeness to nature and unconditional "self-reliance," **Henry David Thoreau** (1817–1862) literally immersed himself in nature in a long-term self-experiment. Young Thoreau lived and worked for some time in Emerson's household and produced texts for the magazine the *Dial*, the voice and mouthpiece of the transcendentalists. His most important contribution to American literature, however, was the autobiographical work *Walden* (1854), which deals with Thoreau's personal experiences during a two-year retreat in a secluded hut at Walden Pond near Concord, Massachusetts.

In literary history, Thoreau's *Walden* presents a milestone of American autobiography. On the one hand, Thoreau adopts elements of this genre, which were first explored by Puritan journals and by Benjamin Franklin. On the other hand, however, he breaks with the Protestant work ethic and introspection of his predecessors. Individual confrontation with nature becomes a catalyst for knowledge and self-realization, as propagated by Emerson's transcendental philosophy. Leaving society and retreating into nature was not uncommon for nineteenth-century Americans. Diverse religious, political, or philosophical theories produced and fueled a large number of dropout-communities, all in want of utopian modes of life. Thoreau's *Walden*, in many ways, seems like a one-man version of these experimental communities, trying to put transcendentalist ideas to the test.

Among the many peculiarities of *Walden* are the long list-like enumerations of the flora, fauna, and topography of Walden Pond's immediate surroundings. The most conspicuous example of Thoreau's compulsive empiricism is the exact survey plan of the lake, which Thoreau also deemed to be important enough to include in his published text. Thoreau believed that, by minutely taking the measurements of the lake, he could show an individual example of cosmic harmony in nature: "If we knew all the laws of Nature, we should

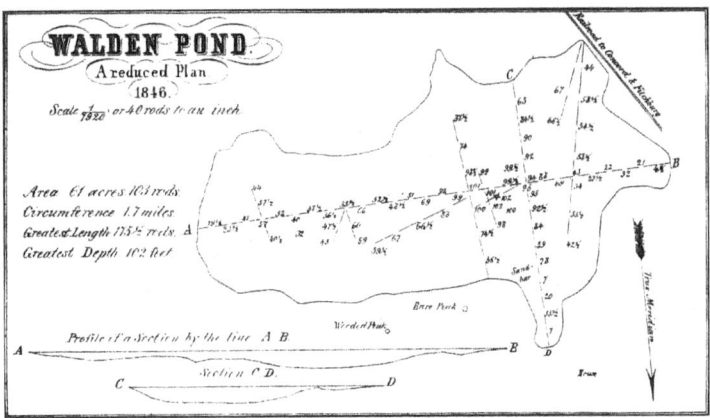

Figure 4.1 Map of Walden Pond (1846) from Henry David Thoreau's *Walden* (1854).

need only one fact, or the description of one actual phenomenon, to infer all the particular results at that point" (338).

With great ease, Thoreau takes his findings about the lake and applies them to other dimensions of existence, when, for example, he concludes: "What I have observed of the pond is no less true in ethics" (339). Many of the text's seeming inconsistencies and peculiarities, including the rather strange measurement of the lake, can be explained by the transcendentalist dichotomy of "understanding" and "reason." For Thoreau, as for all transcendentalists, intense sensual perception (= understanding), here in the form of measurement, is used to arrive at larger insights (= reason), which in turn serve as his stepping-stone to transcend these individual measurements for a vision of the cosmic harmony in nature.

Thoreau is not just influenced by the transcendental mind-set of Emerson. In fact, many passages of *Walden* also show a Protestant work ethic in the Puritan sense, and to some extent remind one of Benjamin Franklin's *Autobiography*. Despite his rebellion against social norms, Thoreau is caught in this long tradition of economic and material aspects of American self-understanding, which is most visible in the painstaking enumeration of all of his financial expenditures during his two-year dropout. Thoreau meant to show how inexpensive his undertaking was, and, by doing so, demonstrated to his readers a kind of self-discipline akin to the work ethic of Benjamin Franklin, manifesting itself in the meticulous accounting of material and spiritual assets.

Politically speaking, the most influential of Thoreau's works are programmatic texts, such as "Resistance to Civil Government" (1849), which in the twentieth century, for instance, influenced opponents of the Vietnam War, as well as Mahatma Gandhi and Martin Luther King. In his essays, Thoreau supports disobedience against State norms or regulations whenever they contradict a person's individual conscience. Thoreau himself, for example, refused to pay taxes for the Mexican-American War (1846–1848) because he found it unjust, and was consequently sent to prison for violating the law. Ultimately, he went as far as questioning every kind of authority, stating in "Resistance to Civil Government": "That government is best which governs least" (385).

Emerson and Thoreau clearly concentrate their self-realization on very general aspects of a human being. The works of their fellow transcendentalist, **Margaret Fuller** (1810–1850), add a female dimension to this entire discussion. Fuller's dominant father raised Margaret according to the standards of a boy's education, in order to turn her into an intellectual child prodigy. In *Memoirs of Margaret Fuller Ossoli* (1852) she will later, in an Emersonian vein, object to this ascribed role, severely criticizing her unnatural education and lonely childhood, devoid of contact with children her own age. Her biggest success as a writer was *Woman in the Nineteenth Century* (1845), in which Fuller, inspired by the *Declaration of Independence*, asks whether the dictum, "all men are created equal," also applies to American women. In doing so, Fuller follows the tradition of French feminist Olympe de Gouges, who, toward the end of the eighteenth century, commented on the idea of equality of the French Revolution by testing its applicability for women. In her feminist critique, Fuller marks the beginning of a long tradition of American feminists who discuss women's roles in larger philosophical or economic contexts, including Charlotte Perkins Gilman toward the end of the nineteenth century.

Another author situated in the vicinity of the transcendentalists – at least geographically speaking – was **Nathaniel Hawthorne** (1804–1864). Being Emerson's neighbor in Concord, Hawthorne was familiar with the ideas of transcendentalism. However, he went his own literary way, despite obvious transcendentalist elements in his works. While Emerson demands an undivided focus on the present, discounting burdens of the past as "sepulchers of the fathers" (7), Hawthorne deliberately positions his texts within American history, including seventeenth-century American Puritanism. He creates highly symbolic and allegorical texts, partly committed to retrogressive aesthetics, which stands in stark contrast to Thoreau, who clearly preferred a more immediate approach to the world around him. Conversely, Hawthorne questions the sensory world, which in turn transcendentalists consider to be the starting point of philosophical inquiry. In order to do justice to his own literary credo, Hawthorne's definition of the literary genre of the romance assigns a central status to the imagination. From a modern perspective, there is hardly any difference between Hawthorne's romance and the traditional novel. For Hawthorne, however, the novel is characterized by a strong emphasis on realism, whereas the romance incorporates dreamlike, allegorical, and supernatural elements, thereby obscuring the borderline between imagination and reality.

Hawthorne's most famous novel, *The Scarlet Letter* (1850), is an impressive example of his literary reorientation. In a long preface to the text, the so-called "Custom House," Hawthorne stylizes himself as the fictional publisher of a found manuscript ("The Scarlet Letter") from the early days of Puritan New England. In this lengthy preface, Hawthorne sketches his theory of fiction, which gravitates around the blurring of fictional genres.

The novel proper tells the story of Hester Prynne, a young woman from Puritan Boston. Convicted for adultery and the birth of an illegitimate daughter, she is put on the scaffold and sentenced to wear the scarlet letter "A," standing for "adultery," on the garments over her breast at all times. She refuses to reveal the identity of her lover, thereby protecting the reputable priest Arthur Dimmesdale. While Hester submits to her role as a social outcast, the priest suffers from his undisclosed sin, developing insurmountable problems, both psychological and physical. Hester's former husband, the physician Roger Chillingworth, by chance guesses Dimmesdale's guilt and starts to torment him under the pretense of medical treatment. As the pressure becomes too much for Dimmesdale to bear, he confesses his affair with Hester Prynne in a public speech at the scaffold. After revealing the letter "A," which had mysteriously developed on his chest like the stigmata of a saint, he dies in Hester's arms. Subsequently, Hester engages in community service but continues to wear the letter "A" on her clothes. The scene with Dimmesdale's "stigmatization," or the disclosure of the wound-like sign, is indicative of the combination of realistic and mythical elements, as well as historical and allegorical features in Hawthorne's romances.

On the one hand, Hawthorne's urge to go back in time to the age of Puritanism is autobiographically motivated, as one of his ancestors was involved in the Salem witchcraft trials. On the other hand, Hawthorne perceives Puritanism as a symbolic and subliminal force in American thinking, necessary to be reviewed. His early texts, such as the short story "The May-Pole of Merry Mount" (1837), already deal with the dark side of Puritanism. It tells the well-known story of Thomas Morton, who got into conflict with the Puritans in seventeenth-century New England because of his nonconformist behavior.

However, despite anchoring many of his concerns in history, Hawthorne also discusses contemporary issues. *The Blithedale Romance* (1852), for example, uses a concrete experiment of the transcendentalists – the so-called Brook Farm community – in a kind of *roman à clef*. He introduces, and mildly ridicules, transcendentalist Margaret Fuller as the feminist character Zenobia in his novel. The book grapples with transcendentalist ideas in order to investigate their potential for sociopolitical realization. As in the majority of his works, the novel also contains an autobiographical dimension, since Hawthorne himself spent time in the Brook Farm community, a private transcendentalist experience he later critically questioned in his romance.

5 American Renaissance

Another group of authors, hardly separable from the transcendentalists, are the writers of the so-called American Renaissance, a name the literary scholar F. O. Matthiessen coined for mid-nineteenth-century literature in the United States. The writers whose work constituted this movement were busy writing a national narrative and interrogating national ideals and the failures of American democracy. Often Emerson, Hawthorne, and Thoreau are also seen as representatives of the American Renaissance. Conversely, authors like **Herman Melville** (1819–1891) are sometimes called transcendentalists. Melville's novels and short stories present a transcendentalist mind-set despite the fact that he was not part of their inner circle.

Melville was the son of a bankrupt merchant and had to stand on his own two feet at the age of 15 in order to financially support the family. At 19, he went to sea and spent several years on whaling ships in the South Pacific. The experiences of these sea voyages partially formed the autobiographical background for his early fiction. Melville's first novel, *Typee* (1846), became the biggest literary success during his lifetime, telling the story of the sailor Tommo, who shares autobiographical features with Melville. After escaping a cruel captain, Tommo finds shelter with an allegedly cannibalistic tribe on one of the Marquesas Islands, where he spends several months in a relationship with a South Sea beauty. However, the paradisiacal harmony is overshadowed by the latently lurking danger of cannibalism and the obligation for facial and body tatooing in order to fully integrate into the culture of the Typee tribe. These fears eventually prompt Tommo to escape and return to the Western world.

Above all in the treatment of tattoos, which Melville knew about from his own stay in the Marquesas Islands, an important dimension of his work is already tangible in his debut novel: his ambivalent personal attitude toward otherness, including both cultural and sexual dimensions. The first-person narrator is drawn to and appalled by the culture of the Typee in a number of ways. In this unfamiliar environment of otherness, the protagonist exhibits a certain homoerotic penchant which, so it seems, can occur only in the context of cultural otherness. The subliminal diction of the first-person narrator is telling when he interacts with men of this foreign culture. Suddenly, the male protagonist adopts the role of a sexually desirable woman or, as Melville in a passage of *Typee* expresses it, the "belle of the season" (195). A number of scholars believe that they see precisely this homoerotic dimension of Melville's thinking at work in his futile strife for personal acknowledgment by Hawthorne, whom he obviously felt rejected by.

His posthumously most successful book, *Moby Dick* (1851), processes these ingredients of his early novels even further: the seafaring setting, the cultural contact, the transcendentalist involvement with nature, and a sexually experimental component. In addition to these elements, the novel, on an allegorical level, negotiates major concerns of the United States at the time. For example, it stylizes the whaling ship *Pequod* under Captain Ahab as a misguided state and reflects on a confluence of destructive forces that were shaping America at the time, including slavery, political authoritarianism, capitalism, westward expansion, and the Mexican-American War. The story is told by the sailor Ishmael, who signs on to a whaling ship under the command of the mysterious Captain Ahab. Ahab, as becomes apparent on the open sea, is obsessed with getting revenge on the white whale Moby Dick, which, in an earlier encounter, had bitten off his leg. What was planned as a commercial whaling trip becomes a chase of the white whale through the seven seas and culminates in Ahab being drawn into the deep of the ocean by the whale.

Interesting from a narratological point of view, as well as groundbreaking, is the use of the sailor Ishmael as narrator, whose voice begins the novel, addressing the readers with the words "Call me Ishmael" (21). Ishmael's perspective, from which he tells Ahab's story, is very unusual, as the reader only learns about the events of the voyage through Ishmael's limited point of view. The reason for this unconventional narrative technique lies in the concomitant mystification of Ahab. Had Melville used Ahab as first-person narrator, his complicated thoughts would no longer be a secret to the reader, but instead would become predictable. In a similar way, F. Scott Fitzgerald will later use this technique in his novel *The Great Gatsby* (1925), where he mystifies his central character Gatsby through the limited first-person narration of an insignificant minor character.

Apart from these narratological characteristics, *Moby Dick* – similar to Thoreau's *Walden* – sets itself apart through a number of meticulous list-like enumerations, in this case from the field of whaling techniques. Again, the reader is reminded of the transcendental "understanding" of empirical facts, which eventually creates a cosmic knowledge in the form of a more comprehensive "reason." But Melville does not stop at these lists. Like Hawthorne's works, *Moby Dick* is full of symbols and parables, most noticeable in Ahab's fight with elemental forces, represented by the white whale.

Melville's main theme of confrontation with the Other, which he first explored in *Typee*, surfaces in manifold ways in *Moby Dick*. On the one hand, it becomes apparent in Ahab's psychic otherness, but, on the other, Melville also introduces the character of the noble savage Queequeg, who, despite being a tattooed bounty hunter, maintains a friendly relationship with Ishmael. Again, a possible homoerotic deep structure crystallizes in this very relationship, when Ishmael, who has to share a bed with Queequeg, metaphorically slips into another sexual identity. As the sleeping Queequeg, who represents cultural otherness, unintentionally puts his arm over Ishmael, the first-person narrator suddenly envisions himself in a female role. "Upon waking next morning about daylight, I found Queequeg's arm thrown over me in the most loving and affectionate manner. You had almost thought I had been his wife" (43).

This kind of otherness that Melville deals with in his seafaring novels also emerges in his short stories, albeit in a different form. In his short story "Bartleby, the Scrivener: A Story of Wall Street" (1856), the first-person narrator, a company owner on New York's Wall Street, meets the shrewd scrivener Bartleby. By eluding societal norms in an extreme way, Bartleby represents a different kind of friction with the Other, this time taking place *within* American culture.

The odd Bartleby becomes a consistent denier of societal norms, answering to all of his employer's orders with an automated "I would prefer not to" (68). The first-person narrator finds himself helplessly at the mercy of this passive resistance and reluctantly has to accept that Bartleby settles down in one of the offices and refuses to carry out any kind of work. Only through relocating the company is the owner finally able to rid himself of Bartleby and resume normal business activities.

In this short story, Melville manages to radically get even with the American Dream of the Puritan work ethic, in the wake of Benjamin Franklin's *Autobiography*. In the character of Bartleby, Melville also gives voice to Thoreau's concept of civil disobedience, while simultaneously pushing the transcendentalist credo to an absurd level. Bartleby's character anticipates, by at least a century, elements of the theater of the absurd or the postmodernist short story in the vein of J. D. Salinger. Melville's overall interest in otherness in his seafaring novels and short stories can be grounded in prevalent general notions of cultural pessimism at the time and Melville's specific interest in the sexual nature of man in particular.

Melville's contemporary **Edgar Allan Poe** (1809–1849) went a step further into this psychology of otherness, as he devoted himself to exploring the dark and deviant side of the human mind. Poe, after the death of his parents, partially raised in England by a merchant from Richmond, quit his law studies in order to pursue a writer's career against his foster father's will. His early short stories received prizes, which in turn secured him employment with literary magazines, including the *Southern Literary Messenger* (1834–1864), in which Poe published numerous reviews, essays, poems, and short stories.

Especially the short stories illustrate Poe's fascination with the dismal, morbid, and abnormal, indulging in macabre and bizarre themes. Being buried alive, returning from the dead, falling into the deep, and even necrophilia are the ingredients of his narratives. In the short story "The Tell-Tale Heart" (1843), for example, the first-person narrator develops a strange fascination with a physical defect of his landlord, which ultimately compels the disturbed narrator to kill the old man. After hiding the dismembered body under the floorboards, and while being questioned by the police about the whereabouts of the old man, the murderer believes he hears the dead man's heartbeat loud and clear.

Unnerved by the imagined sound, the protagonist finally screams out a confession to the startled police. With this anatomy of a pathological murder, or respectively, the inner perspective of the disturbed perpetrator, Poe founded the genre of psychological detective fiction.

Poe is not only interested in the abysmal psyche of the murderer, but also in the mental conditions of victims upon facing imminent death. Poe employs these themes in various tales, for example, in the psychological and physical agonies of the first-person narrator in "The Pit and the Pendulum" (1842). In the dark of a dungeon, the narrator is exposed to various dangers, such as plummeting into a well. The central motif of the story, however, is the protagonist's impending death through an enormous razor-sharp pendulum gradually closing in on the bound man with each move. Through the inner perspective of the victim, Poe explores mental conditions in extreme situations, as well as the psychic mechanisms underlying this kind of mortal fear. The story might remind readers of Charles Brockden Brown's novel *Edgar Huntly*, whose protagonist is equally trapped in the dark of a cave and exposed to dangers such as falling into an abyss. Like Brown, Poe is indebted in many ways to English and German romanticism, for example, the works of E. T. A. Hoffmann and the Gothic novel of the late eighteenth century.

Poe's psychological interests included, besides the perpetrator and the victim, also the detective. In the story "The Murders in the Rue Morgue" (1841), the detective Auguste Dupin has to solve a gruesome murder. Poe is not interested in the conviction of the perpetrator in the sense of the classical "whodunit" scheme. Rather, Poe is absorbed in exemplifying how to deduce meaning from a chain of evidence. The detective's deductions are disclosed only at the end of the story in the form of a bombshell revelation. The readers, who have been identifying with the naive first-person narrator and sidekick to the detective, must in the end realize their own inadequacies in reading the evidence correctly. Poe anticipates the contemporary film genre of so-called "mind-tricking narratives," such as M. Night Shyamalan's *The Sixth Sense* (1999), which reveal at the end of the movie that, up to this point, we as viewers have been severely misinterpreting crucial aspects of the plot. The reader or audience thus slips into the role of a detective who has to decipher the overall significance of certain aspects of the story. Poe classifies this kind of narration as "tales of ratiocination." Because of their particular structure, the actual suspense of these tales lies in the correct way of reading the evidence, whereas solving the case becomes less important. "The Murders in the Rue Morgue" realizes this strategy in an almost parodistic way, when in the end a runaway orangutan turns out to be responsible for the brutal killings. We as readers tended to believe the contradictory accounts of the witnesses, each of which claimed to have heard the murderer speak in a different language. These "languages" turn out to be the sounds made by the raging orangutan that the listeners had mistaken for human utterances in foreign tongues.

Poe's enthusiasm for the analytic is also present in his essays on literary theory. In "The Philosophy of Composition" (1846), Poe claims to have followed strict methodical steps when composing his poem "The Raven" (1845). He argues that all compositional elements work toward the common goal of achieving a "unity of effect" for the reader. From this objective, Poe derives all ensuing steps of composition, such as the brevity of a text in order "to be read at one sitting" (273), or rhythmical and phonetic elements supporting the content level. In emphasizing the unity of a text, Poe anticipates one of the main tenets of the theoretical approaches of New Criticism in the middle of the twentieth century.

Similar to the detective in the "tales of ratiocination," Poe, in his role as the poet in "The Philosophy of Composition," unmasks us as bad readers. Like the all-perceiving detective, Poe, in his superior authorial role, informs us about how to read or interpret the elements of the particular case under investigation. The "case," of course, is not a crime case, supposed to give away its secrets to an investigator, but Poe's poem "The Raven." "The Philosophy of Composition," despite pretending to be an essay on literary theory, upon closer inspection, turns out to be yet another cleverly contrived or concealed "tale of ratiocination."

In the same essay, Poe provides further insight into the macabre logic of his aesthetics when he claims that "the death then of a beautiful woman is unquestionably the most poetical topic in the world" (278). This statement holds a key function for the understanding of a number of eroticizing depictions of dying women in Poe's texts. The most famous example is the short story "Ligeia" (1838), which deals with the death of two women, as well as one woman's mysterious return from the dead. Besides Poe's enthusiasm for scientific deduction in his detective stories, his texts also feature popular semiscientific movements of the time, such as mesmerism, which advocates invisible magnetic ties between animate beings, as well as Swedenborg's cosmic spiritualism, both of which center around connecting to the dead or the sphere of the afterlife.

Poe's American contemporaries received his devotion to the deviant with mixed feelings. Emerson – the doyen of transcendentalism – took little or no pleasure in Poe's texts. This is not surprising since Poe's explorations of the dark side of the human psyche obviously contradict the calculated optimism and utopianism of the transcendentalist project as such. Poe's reception in Europe was fundamentally different. Especially his admirers in France, Charles Baudelaire and Stéphane Mallarmé, indirectly caused a more positive assessment of Poe in the United States in the long run.

In general, audiences in the middle of the nineteenth century preferred more traditional prose texts. The plot structure of the sentimental novel of the late eighteenth and early nineteenth centuries, with its melodramatic black-and-white stereotyping, continued to be very popular. Susan Warner's (1819–1858) bestselling novel *The Wide, Wide World* (1850) and Maria Susanna Cummins's (1827–1866) *The Lamplighter* (1854) are representative of this extremely popular strain of nineteenth-century sentimental literature that has received much attention from scholars over the last twenty years. The best example is **Harriet Beecher Stowe**'s (1811–1896) *Uncle Tom's Cabin* (1852), which ultimately became the most popular American novel of the nineteenth century. From her white Calvinist background, Stowe produced the most influential novel before the Civil War, which Abraham Lincoln is said to have called "the book that made this great war." Whether an authentic statement or simply lore, it pinpoints the role that Stowe's text had in setting the abolitionist cause in motion in the middle of the nineteenth century.

The story evolves around Uncle Tom, a faithful, almost saint-like, slave who is separated from his wife and children when he is sold to a cruel Yankee. As Tom refuses, even when being whipped, to reveal the whereabouts of two escaped slaves, he dies as a result of the mistreatment. The young former owner, George Shelby, who traveled to

Tom's rescue, cannot save the dying man, but solemnly swears to campaign for the abolition of slavery.

Despite Stowe's obvious impact on the abolitionist cause and the emotional mobilization before the American Civil War, Tom's characterization remains problematic. Passively tolerating any kind of injustice, Tom becomes the stereotypical abstraction of the "good nigger," who bears all mistreatments of himself and his people with submissive subordination. In his death, he is stylized as a Christ-like savior of his race, causing white American culture to fundamentally reevaluate its racial positions. It is not by chance that the term "Uncle Tom" has become a synonym for a submissive and assimilated African American who lacks any kind of personal agency for himself or his race.

In the second half of the nineteenth century, Stowe's novel was – without her consent – performed again and again in various stage adaptations, becoming one of the most popular dramas in nineteenth-century America. Especially the novel's melodramatic features were predestined for the taste in drama at that time. Similar ingredients can be found in other plays from this era, for example, in the mulatto drama *The Octoroon* (1859) by the Irish melodramatist **Dion Boucicault** (1820–1890), who drafted plays specifically for the American market. At the center of the play is an "octoroon," that is, a woman of one-eighth African blood. Despite her absolutely white appearance, she is, under the current law, to be considered black and thus sold as a slave at an auction. The play's clear oppositions between good and evil, together with the sentimental plot of racial passing, delighted audiences. However, both texts, *Uncle Tom's Cabin* and *The Octoroon*, are written by authors who are not part of the oppressed minority for which they speak. In both cases the reader encounters only clichéd, passive characters who pose no real danger to the prevalent white supremacy.

Already in the eighteenth century, however, African Americans had raised their voices in so-called "slave narratives." An early example is **Olaudah Equiano** (*c.*1745–1797), who with *The Interesting Narrative of the Life of Olaudah Equinano, or Gustavus Vassa, the African* (1789) laid the foundation for the tradition of African-American autobiography. Equiano narrates incidents after having been abducted by slave hunters as an 11-year-old in West Africa, his passage to America, his life as a slave, and how he eventually managed to buy his freedom. Recent scholarship has been able to point out fictional elements in Equiano's autobiographical narrative. For example, the first part of the text that relates Equiano's boyhood in Africa might be invented since external documents support the fact that he was actually born and raised in North America. Irrespective of the question of authenticity, these older slave narratives like Equiano's mostly focus on the passage from the African homeland into the New World as well as the ensuing acculturation process. Nineteenth-century authors, on the other hand, concentrate on the circumstances of a slave's individual everyday life and the chain of events leading to the person's emancipation from slavery. Composed in this spirit, the autobiography *Narrative of the Life of Frederick Douglass, an American Slave* by the literate runaway slave **Frederick Douglass** (1818–1895), became an immediate bestseller after its publication in 1845. In a similar vein, **Harriet Jacobs**'s (1813–1897) *Incidents in the Life of a Slave Girl* (1861) lent power to the intensifying African-American voice in autobiographies.

American literature during the middle of the century found its own voice in prose and in the genre of poetry, which underwent significant changes under the auspices of transcendentalism. With his 1855 poetry edition of *Leaves of Grass*, school dropout, autodidact, printer, and publicist **Walt Whitman** (1819–1892) managed to express transcendentalist ideas in a completely new format, and, at the same time, revolutionized American poetry like no other before or after him.

Similar to Thoreau, Whitman followed Emerson's dogma of self-experience, which is fed by an individual's immediate interaction with her or his surroundings. While Thoreau ascribes a special significance to nature, Whitman goes several steps further. His poems not only include nature in the sense of the animated world that surrounds us, but he expands the Emersonian concept of nature to *all* aspects of life, including material culture. Casting himself in the role of the American bard, Whitman aspires to romantic notions of the poet as an advocate for all people. In list-like chants Whitman celebrates all possible manifestations of life, American life in particular. In his preface to *Leaves of Grass*, Whitman states: "The Americans of all nations at any time upon the earth have probably the fullest poetical nature. The United States themselves are essentially the greatest poem" (5). Consequently, America has to manifest itself in him, because as the

American Renaissance 53

Figure 5.1 Portrait of Walt Whitman (1854) by Samuel Hollyer of a daguerreotype by Gabriel Harrison, frontispiece of the first edition of *Leaves of Grass* (1855).

American bard he "incarnates its geography and natural life and rivers and lakes" (7). In this cosmic function, Whitman sees himself as the people's transcendental mediator between nature and intellect, the one "to indicate the path between reality and their souls" (10). His program is reminiscent of Emerson's call for an American Homer, who is supposed to grip the country like the Greek bard in an all-encompassing account of its current culture. It is thus not surprising that Emerson, as one of the few readers of the first edition of *Leaves of Grass*, encouraged Whitman and his project in a letter: "I find it the most extraordinary piece of wit and wisdom that America has yet contributed" (ix). How important the legitimization by the period's most important American thinker and his intellectual father figure was for Whitman, becomes apparent in the fact that Whitman, in all following editions of *Leaves of Grass*, printed Emerson's full letter along with his own preface.

Whitman's overall agenda, as this American bard, becomes evident in the first lines of "Song of Myself," the opening poem in the first edition of *Leaves of Grass*:

> I celebrate myself, and sing myself,
> And what I assume you shall assume,
> For every atom belonging to me as good belongs to you.
>
> I loafe and invite my soul,
> I lean and loafe at my ease observing a spear of summer
>   grass.
>
> My tongue, every atom of my blood, form'd from this soil,
>   this air,
> Born here of parents born here from parents the same, and
>   their parents the same.

(1–7)

The opening verses of the poem resume the concept of incarnation, which Whitman expounded in the preface. Within the American bard, the lines between subject and object become blurred. Everything merges with the cosmic nature of the poet, and in reverse, the poet merges with the cosmic of nature. In his holistic view of the world, which does away with the idea of difference, Whitman's text is reminiscent of Emerson's "transparent eye-ball," trying to absorb his environment into himself as an act of universal incorporation.

Whitman, however, took his poetry further than his transcendentalist role model Emerson had probably envisioned the American bard ever to take this project. He continued Emerson's transcendentalist idea of nature in the most conspicuous and revolutionary way in an ongoing attempt to reassess *human* nature. Whitman glorifies the human body, especially its sexuality, picking up threads of his predecessors, such as Emerson, Thoreau, and especially Melville. However, he weaves them into a radically new fabric of a pansexual texture, stylizing homosexuality and heterosexuality as the holistic nature of human beings. In "From Pent-up Aching Rivers" (1860) he writes:

> From my own voice resonant, singing the phallus,
> Singing the song of procreation,
> Singing the need of superb children and therein superb
>   grown people,
> Singing the muscular urge and the blending,
> Singing the bedfellow's song.
>
> (4–8)

"Spontaneous Me" (1856), in a similar spirit, celebrates sexuality in all its corporeal facets:

> Love-thoughts, love-juice, love-odor, love-yielding, love-
>   climbers, and the climbing sap,
> Arms and hands of love, lips of love, phallic thumb of love,
>   breasts of love, bellies press'd and glued together with
>   love
> Earth of chaste love, life that is only life after love,
> The body of my love, the body of the woman I love, the
>   body of the man, the body of the earth.
>
> (12–15)

Whitman's incantation of pansexuality, with all the dimensions of heterosexuality and homosexuality, goes far beyond what was imaginable in traditional poetry up to that point. Whitman thereby was to inspire twentieth-century poets, including the Spanish writer García Lorca and the Beat poet Allen Ginsberg.

In contrast to Whitman's extroverted position, his contemporary **Emily Dickinson** (1830–1886) seems, at first sight, to venture into the exact opposite direction, isolating herself from her environment and the external world. Dickinson came from a renowned family of lawyers and politicians in Amherst, Massachusetts, whose heritage reached back to Puritan New England. In accordance with her social status, she received a good education, being relatively well integrated in the social activities of her respected family in her early years. As she got older, Dickinson, who remained unmarried, withdrew more and more from public life. Her sphere of action was limited to the family house and the attached garden in Amherst. Even within the family estate, Dickinson maintained contact with visitors only indirectly through the gap of a door left slightly ajar when entertaining them.

In the second half of her life, corresponding with her withdrawal from social contact, Dickinson wrote about 1,800 poems, only half a dozen of which were published during her lifetime. Despite engaging in close epistolary exchanges with Dickinson, publishers and critics did not recognize the innovative potential of Dickinson's poetry. Only after her death, a large number of self-bound booklets of poetry were found in her room. Dickinson's sister was responsible for the poems' first publication a few years after Emily's death. However, a number of "corrections" made by the publishers distorted the innovative nature and originality of her message. Furthermore, her poems were received rather cautiously until the 1930s. It was New Criticism in the middle of the twentieth century and feminist literary studies in later decades that eventually ascribed to Dickinson a position equal to Emerson, Thoreau, and Whitman as a major voice in American literature.

What distinguishes Dickinson's poetry? Contrary to the public voices of her time, such as Walt Whitman's, Emily Dickinson's *oeuvre* is directed inward, focused, concentrated, and condensed. While Whitman extols America in its unity of nature, geography, material culture, and its inhabitants by seemingly abandoning traditional verse and meter, Dickinson bundles her vision as if through an introspective looking glass. Many of her poems use very unconventional imagery, reminiscent of the conceits of the Metaphysical poets of the seventeenth century, or the symbolism of the Puritans that we have seen in the language of the poet Edward Taylor. Dickinson's poem "My Life had stood – a Loaded Gun," for instance, features such a far-fetched metaphor, typical of this religiously motivated poetic tradition:

> My Life had stood – a Loaded Gun –
> In Corners – till a Day
> The Owner passed – identified –
> And carried Me away –
>
> (1–4)

Dickinson's conceit-like imagery compares the life of the lyrical "I" with a loaded gun. Also typical of Dickinson is her use of a traditional ballad stanza, which is composed of four lines and the rhyme scheme ABCB. Despite these rather conventional features, she uses very intriguing and untypical capitalization and punctuation. How important these punctuation marks and typographic aspects in general were for Dickinson, becomes apparent in her strong reaction to one of the few poems that she published during her lifetime. She complained bitterly that, by inserting additional commas and periods, the publisher had completely changed the meaning of the entire poem.

In Dickinson's poetry, the author's inner world clearly substitutes for the external one. In a multitude of her texts consciousness becomes spatialized, such as in the poem "I felt a Funeral, in my Brain":

> I felt a Funeral, in my Brain,
> And Mourners to and fro
> Kept treading – treading – till it seemed
> That Sense was breaking through –
>
> (1–4)

This example illustrates Dickinson's obsession with death and transience, which is also visible as a determining factor in her letters of the second half of her life.

Besides the unconventional imagery of inner life, typographical idiosyncrasies, and the subject of death, many of Dickinson's poems share an unidentified "master"-figure, often addressed as "signor" or "sir." It is hard to say whether this is a real person of reference, or, and this seems more plausible, a composite imagined figure, in the sense of being a character that assumes different roles in her microcosmos, from lover to Christian savior. For example, in poem 754, "My Life had stood – a Loaded Gun," she calls the owner of her life "My Master." This "master," however, can also more concretely become "God" as in the poem "Over the fence":

> Over the fence –
> Strawberries – grow –
> Over the fence –
> I could climb – if I tried, I know –
> Berries are nice!
>
> But – if I stained my Apron –
> God would certainly scold!
> Oh, dear, – I guess if He were a Boy –
> He'd – climb – if He could!

This poem, ostensibly connoting sexual innuendos, touches on a number of elements that are unique to Dickinson's poetic microcosm. Imaginary barriers that are impossible to overcome, an often recurring garden imagery, as well as the superior master character, are key features of Dickinson's indirect way of coming to terms with questions of patriarchal oppression and sexuality. In this particular case she identifies the figure as "God," but at the same time seems, almost blasphemously, to be questioning God's sexual identity: "I guess if He were a Boy," as opposed to being a female. Of course, "if He were a Boy" could also mean that if God was not grown up yet and still a boy, he would have similar urges as expressed in the poem. In either case, Dickinson departs drastically from conventional religious poetry of the American tradition that her texts, at least at face value, keep evoking.

Especially with this unidentified instance of authority, acting as a regulator, but not as a specific point of reference, Dickinson seems to anticipate postmodern features and elements of the absurd. Furthermore, Dickinson appears to be ahead of her time in regard to the materiality of the sign. Concerned with typography as an integral and meaningful dimension, Dickinson's texts foreshadow aspects of the concrete poetry of e. e. cummings in twentieth-century modernism. It is thus not surprising that the more archaic elements of Dickinson's poetry, such as the conceit-like metaphors, possible relics from American Puritanism, appealed to modernist avant-garde writers. In a famous 1920 essay, T. S. Eliot attributes to the imagery of the Metaphysical poets of the seventeenth century a high potential for modernist poetry. Thus, Dickinson becomes a belatedly appropriated forerunner of modernism and postmodernism, paradoxically pointing back to the Puritan roots of American literature, while simultaneously anticipating modernist stylistic features and twentieth-century modes of psychoanalytic introspection.

6 Gilded Age – Realism

Even though Emily Dickinson's poems of the 1860s seemingly pointed ahead toward modernism and surrealism, the novel of the second half of the nineteenth century in the United States was – at least on the surface – conventional and realistic. Mark Twain mockingly called this literary period the "Gilded Age." It implies an allegedly Golden Age, which, upon closer inspection, turns out to be only gilded on the surface and is, in fact, hollowed out by growing capitalism and materialism. It is the time of the monopolized capital of the Rockefellers, Carnegies, and Mellons, who were able to establish themselves in new industries, such as the extraction of raw materials, the railroad, or telecommunication. At the same time, the Civil War between the North and the South (1861–1865) became the worst sociopolitical rupture in American history. Interestingly enough, this wound in American identity left conspicuously little traces in the literary productions of the time.

Mark Twain (1835–1910) is one of the few authors who addressed the antagonism between the North and the South in his works. Born as Samuel Langhorne Clemens, he grew up in the South. At the age of 12, he left school, working on river steamers for several years and struggling as a traveling printer. Twain fought on the side of the Confederacy, but soon deserted, spending the rest of the Civil War out West. During this time, he worked as a journalist and assumed the pseudonym Mark Twain, under which he later gained international publicity and fame. "Mark twain" is a phrase called out by river pilots to signal the depth of two fathoms, that is, safe passage in deep enough waters.

One of Twain's first publications, a collection of short stories called *The Celebrated Jumping Frog of Calaveras County* (1867), turned out to be overwhelmingly successful and laid the foundation for his future reputation. The eponymous title story, on a small scale, already encapsulates the central elements of Twain's later prose. It is a so-called "tall tale," a kind of cock-and-bull story, which is part of the folklore narratives of the American Southwest: an educated gentleman meets a clever local hero and the interaction between the two character types creates a situational comedy. Alleged civilized superiority and backwoods shrewdness compete with one another, just like Standard English and regional dialect. James Russell Lowell, one of the most influential literary commentators of the time, praised Mark Twain's story for ingeniously combining local narrative traditions with literary elements of satire and irony. In the title story, a narrator recounts the humorous tale of Jim Smiley, who trains a frog until it wins all frog high-jump contests. Eventually, a friend dupes Smiley by feeding the frog lead-shot pellets, thus impairing its ability to jump and win the contest.

Many of these humoristic elements can also be found in Twain's successful novels, such as *The Adventures of Huckleberry Finn* (1884). What at first seems to be a nostalgic reminiscence of happy childhood days becomes, upon closer inspection, a multilayered analysis of American culture and America's racial problems. The novel's narrator is Huck Finn, who, due to his lack of education and his status as a quasi-orphan, has a rather unconventional outlook on his environment. He teams up with the runaway slave Jim, with whom he spends considerable time on the run, going south on a raft on the Mississippi River. Especially Twain's use of Huck as narrator is groundbreaking, as the story is told from the unconventional first-person perspective of a social outcast. Twain even realistically reproduces the protagonist's sociolect, which deviates drastically from conventional usage in grammar, style, and pronunciation. Despite his temporal distance from the transcendentalists, Huck functions as a hidden voice for Emerson's fresh, unobstructed, natural view of the world. Huck is not weighed down by any burdens of civilization, and thus is able to approach his environment with unspoiled immediacy. Due to his lack of education and his informal upbringing, Huck also lacks culturally acquired racial stereotypes, a disposition which lets him interact with Jim in an immediate and unbiased manner.

62 Gilded Age – Realism

HUCKLEBERRY FINN.

Figure 6.1 Illustration by Edward Winsor Kemble for the first edition of *Huckleberry Finn* (1884).

Huck Finn's character not only points back to transcendentalism, but also reflects major trends of the period through its realistic depiction of the language and the thoughts of an uneducated social underling. Realism, toward the end of the nineteenth century, becomes the dominant force in the American novel, but Twain points even further into the future, anticipating and influencing the modernist literature of the first decades of the twentieth century. Novels in the 1920s will take Twain's limited perspective of an outcast even further, as, for example, William Faulkner's *The Sound and the Fury*, which renders part of the story from the perspective of a severely mentally handicapped person.

Huck Finn has been polarizing audiences until today, not least because of the realistically depicted illiteracy of the narrator. Above all, pre-Civil War race problems, as they are portrayed in Huck and Jim's relationship, proved to be explosive. The novel has often been banned from libraries, or was criticized for its stereotypical depiction of the African-American Jim and Huck's interaction with him. However, it is often overlooked that Twain, despite the use of terms such as "nigger," meant to present an unbiased encounter between blacks and whites.

Experimenting with unusual points of view through unconventional narrator figures is not restricted to *Huck Finn*. In *Call of the Wild* (1903), Twain's contemporary **Jack London** (1876–1916) tells the story from the point of view of a sled dog called Buck:

> Buck did not read the newspaper or he would have known that trouble was brewing, ... Because men, groping in the Arctic darkness, had found a yellow metal, and ... thousands of men were rushing into the Northland. These men wanted dogs.
>
> (15–16)

In the end, after a number of degrading tasks and heroic deeds for different masters, Buck wins his freedom as he advances to be the leader of a pack of wolves in the Alaskan wilderness.

Despite the unconventional point of view, *Call of the Wild* highlights numerous themes of Jack London's other work, most of which are autobiographically motivated. Young Jack, too, lived through an eventful youth, in which he came into conflict with the law several times. After some years at sea – an experience that strongly influenced his novel *The Sea Wolf* (1904) – the autodidact London followed the gold rush to the Klondike in Alaska. London, who was interested and engaged in social matters, became a wealthy and renowned man, later retiring to a vast California estate. However, despite international fame and material success, London was never really pleased with himself or his life situation.

Both Jack London's, and even more so Mark Twain's, works emanate on various levels the call for a faithful depiction of reality in literature – a goal that is commonly referred to as realism. This concern of the late nineteenth century culminates in the American writer and literary theorist **William Dean Howells** (1891–1920), who called the contemporary British novelistic tradition outdated and obsolete.

In his manifesto-like program *Criticism and Fiction* (1891), Howells demands that the novel reorient itself, using the quotidian and ordinary as its models. Howells implicitly negates Hawthorne's concept of the romance, which propagated, for example, supernatural elements and misrepresentations of reality, as the main pillars of fiction.

Howells's list of prerequisites for the realist novel encompasses untypified characters, a simplification of language, nonmelodramatic plots without a standard happy ending, as well as a reduced authorial voice, emphasizing "showing" over "telling." Howells himself tried to incorporate these elements into his own novels, such as *The Rise of Silas Lapham* (1885). Howells introduces the figure of a social climber who manages, through his independent efforts, to rise to economic success. This new character type will resurface with slight variations in subsequent modern American novels.

As the editor of the renowned magazine the *Atlantic Monthly*, Howells also engaged in an extended network with a number of other contemporary authors. Among them was **Henry James** (1843–1916), whose works Howells praised in one of his essays as the paradigm of innovative realist narration. This is remarkable since James, due to the upper-class setting of his novels, digresses considerably from Howells's doctrine of ordinary life. However, in other aspects, such as the privileging of characterization and the emphasis of a new style of showing, James fully answered to the demands of Howell's realism.

Henry James, offspring of a wealthy American family, was mainly educated by private tutors and later attended schools in European cities, including Paris, Geneva, and Bonn. After a year at Harvard Law School, James, inspired by Howells and others, decided to start a career in writing. During this time, he published his first reviews and essays in Howells's *Atlantic Monthly*. James spent the major part of his life in Europe, cultivating an extensive literary exchange with the great writers of realism and naturalism, including Ivan Turgenev, Gustave Flaubert, and Émile Zola. After twenty-one years abroad, James returned to the United States in 1904 as a celebrated author.

Henry James's personal experience with American and European cultures clearly influenced his novels, which often gravitated around issues of cultural contact. Interestingly enough, James preferred to project this acculturation process in his novels onto young female protagonists, like Isabel Archer in *The Portrait of a Lady* (1881), or Daisy

Miller in the eponymous novel of 1878. Again and again, young American women with little experience come into conflict with, to them, unknown and thus seducing European culture, generally represented by a polished and seemingly refined male character. Isabel Archer, a young American with considerable inherited wealth, rejects several serious marriage offers in order to retain her personal independence. Eventually, however, she falls for the European refinement of the impostor Gilbert Osmond. Too late, Isabel figures out that Osmond's alleged interest in her was solely motivated by financial avarice. When already his wife, she finds herself trapped in a marriage that restricts her freedom to decide for herself.

In his novels of manners, Henry James addresses the long tradition of European etiquette as a trap for American heroines who consider themselves to lack this cultural finesse. His naive American protagonists do not adequately read the hollowness of superficially employed European manners, confusing them with moral integrity. It is precisely in the tension between manners and morals that Henry James positions the central characters of his novels.

Besides this moral and culture-specific dimension, Henry James's *oeuvre* demonstrates an unconventional and consequent form of realism. James is especially interested in how human consciousness processes sensory impressions into experience. For James, realism is not only a question of a realistic depiction of reality, but also of realistically showing how sensory perceptions are being processed. James, in comparison to other realists, goes one step further in the direction of a mental or physiological realism that is inevitably reflected in his unconventional writing style. Similar to the characters in his novels, the reader is exposed to the learning process of experience. James tries to have the reader participate in the perception of his characters, without interposing a narrative voice as filter or explicator. For James, realism is a matter of realistically visualizing or representing streams of observation. Characters in the novel, akin to us as readers of the novel, have to read significance into and derive meaning from the sensory data presented, as both are confronted with these impressions without explanatory narrative interventions. James makes this narrative peculiarity possible by using a newly developed narrative perspective, describing a person's state of consciousness from a so-called figural point of view. Traditionally, this inner perspective required a first-person narrative; James, however, renders this relative closeness to the protagonist in a third-person narration. This specific inner perspective creates a certain distance from the protagonist, partly alienating the character from the reader while still maintaining a relatively high degree of intimacy. Franz Stanzel, the founder of modern narratology, uses a passage from James's short story "The Jolly Corner" (1908) as a paradigmatic example of this narrative perspective:

> He always caught the first effect of the steel point of his stick on the old marble of the hall pavement, large black-and-white squares that he remembered as the admiration of his childhood and that had then made in him, as he now saw, for the growth of an early conception of style. This effect was the dim reverberating tinkle as of some far-off bell hung who should say where? – in the depths of the house, of the past, of that mystical other world that might have flourished for him had he not, for weal or woe, abandoned it.
>
> (803)

The detailed descriptions in James's novels present themselves without any further explanatory comment, thus posing a real challenge for the readers, as they have to autonomously form coherent meaning from strings of single observations. For the uninitiated, not much seems to happen in James's fiction, which at times leads unprepared readers to find his work boring or tedious.

While the unconventional realism of Henry James circles around the inner world of the characters, American naturalists tend to turn toward outer circumstances. This movement, partially influenced by journalism, focuses on the milieu as an object of realistic depiction. **Stephen Crane**'s (1871–1900) *Maggie: A Girl of the Streets* (1893) becomes the paradigm for this new approach. It depicts reality through emphatic descriptions of desolate family backgrounds, alcohol abuse, and domestic violence. Maggie, the protagonist, hopes to escape these problems through a relationship with a bartender, but eventually ends up sliding into prostitution and suicide.

Crane's second novel *The Red Badge of Courage* (1895) alternates the setting of urban slums with the battlefields of the American Civil War. The soldier Henry Fleming enthusiastically enters the army, but during his first contact with the enemy becomes disillusioned and disoriented. He deserts his battalion, wanders about the woods in a state of confusion for a long period of time, and eventually returns to his unit. By impressionistically highlighting the perception and mental impact of war atrocities, *The Red Badge of Courage* is reminiscent of Henry James's interest in psychological realism.

Generally speaking, however, American naturalism focuses on the deterministic function of specific conditions of society, including social Darwinism, sexuality, capitalism, and consumption. Although such factors have always been part of plotlines, they now dominate the literature of the late nineteenth century, almost making them a trademark of the period. **Frank Norris** (1870–1902) explores capitalist America, discussing monopolization in his novel *The Octopus: A Story of California* (1901), and the fetishization of money in *McTeague* (1899). **Theodore Dreiser**'s (1871–1945) novel *Sister Carrie* (1900) deals with the new consumer society of the turn of the century in the United States in a slightly different manner. Through the female protagonist Carrie, a rising stage actress, Dreiser manages to capture the spirit of the new urban America with its glamorous department stores and hotel culture. Dreiser's anatomy of American material culture set the tone for a number of modernist novels in the first half of the twentieth century to explore similar topics.

Female protagonists clearly dominate the novels of male writers at the turn of the century, but also more and more female authors use heroines in order to deal with their particularly female or feminist agendas. This tradition goes back to mid-nineteenth-century authors, including **Louisa May Alcott** (1832–1888), the daughter of the transcendentalist Amos Bronson Alcott. Her fiction already proposes strong female characters, who are able to subvert patriarchal standards. For example, in the novella *Behind a Mask, or A Woman's Power* (1866), Louisa May Alcott empowers her heroine, a middle-aged governess, with the ability to pass as a young woman, to outwit male family members, and eventually to marry the widowed father of the family.

Toward the end of the nineteenth century, **Kate Chopin** (1851–1904) in *The Awakening* (1899) imagines a much more differentiated protagonist of uncompromising female self-realization. A holiday affair awakens a new self-confidence in Edna Pontillier, a wife and mother of two children. Ultimately, Edna frees herself of traditional Victorian role models and female clichés, gaining financial independence through her painting. She leaves her family in order to begin a sexual relationship with another man, but entangled in her sense of responsibility, she soon returns to her children. In the end, trapped by the constraints of society, in a gesture of liberation, she commits suicide by swimming out into the open sea.

Another example of female rebellion against patriarchal structures is **Charlotte Perkins Gilman**'s (1860–1935) short story "The Yellow Wallpaper" (1890). Suffering from postpartum depression, the unnamed main character has to succumb to a strict rest cure prescribed by her husband, who also acts as her physician. This treatment completely isolates her from the world, limiting her range of action to a single room and depriving her of any kind of activity, including reading and writing. Eventually, the therapy causes hallucinations, making the protagonist see a woman trapped in the ornaments of her room's yellow wallpaper, desperately trying to free herself from her decorative confinement. As the protagonist's state of mind worsens, she starts to scratch the yellow wallpaper off the wall with her fingernails in order to liberate the woman who is seemingly imprisoned by the outlines of the design. The wallpaper with its ornaments thus becomes a metaphor for Victorian femininity, which equally trapped women as ornamental objects in a patriarchal society.

Gilman not only deals with the role of women from a literary point of view, but in her books *Women and Economics* (1898) and *The Home* (1903) also analyzes concepts of femininity from a socioeconomic perspective. The parallels are remarkable between the literary characterization of the female as a grotesque ornament in "The Yellow Wallpaper" and the sociological analysis of the role of women as a heterogeneous construct in *The Home*. Femininity, for Gilman, counteracts the very principle of division of labor and specialization that allows men to excel in one particular career path of their choice:

> The currents of home-life are so many, so diverse, so contradictory, that they are only maintained by using the woman as a sort of universal solvent; and this position of holding many diverse elements in solution is not compatible with the orderly crystallisation of any of them, or with much peace of mind to the unhappy solvent.
> (152)

Gilman's sociopolitical interest in femininity continues in her utopian novel *Herland* (1912). Published in serial installments in her magazine the *Forerunner*, it serves as Gilman's model of an ideal community of women. Gilman adopts the genre of social utopia, which was very productive in the second half of the nineteenth century, and approaches it from a feminist perspective. In the nineteenth century, the most influential utopian novels employ Marxist and socialist ideas, such as **Edward Bellamy**'s (1850–1898) *Looking Backward: 2000–1887* (1888). Gilman's *Herland*, however, uses the genre as a projection screen for gender-specific considerations. Her book is set in a secluded region of South America where a group of Americans encounter an Amazon-like, strictly female society, which has existed for centuries with no contact with males. Gilman's novel, rediscovered by literary scholars in the second half of the twentieth century, had tremendous influence on the development of feminist utopias and science fiction.

Female writing around the turn of the century, however, did not have to be straightforwardly feminist, as the *oeuvre* of the novelist **Edith Wharton** (1862–1937) demonstrates. Wharton's focus lies on etiquette and the differences between European and American manners, reminding one of Henry James's novels. While the characters of feminist authors usually break away from patriarchal role models in an ostensive way, Lily Bart, the protagonist of Wharton's *The House of Mirth* (1905), more or less remains within the confines of her role – a decorative object of male desire. As a plaything for the New York upper-class marriage market, penniless Lily Bart is not able to strategically use her beauty as her greatest asset. Failing in the economy of female self-marketing, she eventually drops out of the upper circles and dies impoverished. Edith Wharton's work spans several decades, her last novels being published as late as the 1930s, the heyday of modernist fiction. Thematically, as well as stylistically, however, Wharton is committed to writing in the tradition of the novel of manners, for the most part resisting the narratological innovations of modernism at the beginning of the twentieth century.

7 Modernism

Contrary to Wharton, who, despite the fact that she wrote most of her *oeuvre* in the twentieth century, is stylistically and thematically bound to the realist tradition, some turn-of-the-century authors, such as **Ambrose Bierce** (1842–1913), partially predate modernism's narrative experiments by decades. In the short story "An Occurrence at Owl Creek Bridge" (1890), Bierce toys with time and space, two dimensions that hold a central position in early twentieth-century aesthetics. The main character of the story is Peyton Farquhar, a soldier in the American Civil War, who awaits his execution on a railroad bridge, the noose already around his neck. While falling, Farquhar feels how the rope rips, as a consequence of which he dives into the river underneath the bridge and is able to escape his pursuers. The rest of the story gives a detailed account of his flight, up to the point where he returns to his home, falling dead tired into the arms of his wife:

> As he is about to clasp her he feels a stunning blow upon the back of the neck; a blinding white light blazes all about him with a sound like the shock of a cannon – then all is darkness and silence!
>
> Peyton Farquhar was dead; his body, with a broken neck, swung gently from side to side beneath the timbers of the Owl Creek bridge.
>
> (313)

In the last sentences of the story, it becomes apparent to the reader that major parts of the plot, covering several hours of the alleged escape, actually take place only during a split second before the protagonist's death while he is falling. By stretching time, like in a dream, before the rope breaks his neck, Farquhar imagines a detailed getaway spanning an entire day.

Bierce's short story misleads us, similar to the way Edgar Allan Poe's tales of ratiocination set up the reader. We receive the key for making sense out of the plot only at the very end of the narrative, when we realize that we have actually missed major clues within the text. Bierce points – as does Poe – in the direction of early twenty-first-century narrative structures in Hollywood cinema à la *Sixth Sense*, where an epiphany-like end retrospectively puts the plot in a completely new light. An unbroken interest in the use of relative time has excited audiences until today, as, for example, in Christopher Nolan's movie *Inception* (2010), which also plays with experienced time in relation to real time. Bierce's psychological dimension and experimental time structure in "An Occurrence at Owl Creek Bridge" anticipate central aspects of modernism in the first decades of the twentieth century.

Scholarship often refers to modernism as the "era of time and space" because it intensely occupies itself with these two parameters of human experience. In the late nineteenth and early twentieth century, groundbreaking inventions in material culture reshaped people's way of thinking with respect to these two dimensions. In the realm of transportation, steamboats, trains, automobiles, and airplanes seemingly diminished great distances – as did the telegraph and the telephone in communications. Also, new media like photography and film greatly altered the general perception of reality. It is therefore no surprise that the literary practice of the modernist era reflected, experimented with, and revolutionized the use of spatial and temporal aspects of narratives. This goes hand in hand with a strong general interest in mental and psychological processes at the time. Bierce continues Poe's concern with the psychological mechanisms of extreme mental states, yet at the same time anticipates Sigmund Freud's concerns with the psychology of dreams and the imagination.

New technological forms of representation, such as photography and the possibility to depict movement in film, greatly influenced modernist art and literature. Painting, the old privileged medium in the visual arts, received input through cinematic inventions like editing and montage with their new possibilities for rapidly changing perspectives.

New movements in the visual arts, such as cubism, then in turn became modes of inspiration for literary innovation.

One writer, experimenting with photography, film, and avant-garde art à la Cézanne and Picasso, is **Gertrude Stein** (1874–1946). Stein, an expatriate American writer, turned her Paris apartment into

Figure 7.1 Portrait of Gertrude Stein (1906) by Pablo Picasso.

a meeting place for the artistic elite from literature and the visual arts at the beginning of the twentieth century. In this highly creative context, Stein absorbed influences from Picasso, the major visual artist of the time, and, in turn, functioned as a catalyst for a number of young American writers who later became leading proponents of literary modernism, including Hemingway, Fitzgerald, Pound, and Eliot.

Many of Gertrude Stein's texts attempt to render Pablo Picasso's analytic cubism in literary discourse, as, for instance, in "Melanctha," one of the three biographies in her 1909 novel *Three Lives*. Stein uses a narrative style that is characterized by extreme repetitions on a lexical and syntactical level. In addition to reiterating words and parts of sentences with only slight alterations, she often repeats whole paragraphs in the text. As Cubist painters capture multiperspectival aspects of an object on the canvas, Stein tries to create similarly fragmented perspectives in literature. For example, the passage "Rose laughed when she was happy but she had not the wide, abandoned laughter that makes the warm broad glow of negro sunshine" (59–60) appears three times in the text on pages 59, 64, and 77 with only minimal modifications. Similarly, Cubist paintings would render an object with slight modifications several times on one canvas, each time only minimally changing the perspectival vantage point. Cubists thereby simultaneously fuse different moments in time or points in space into one composite image.

Despite her leading role in American modernist literature and her great influence on other important modernists, Stein's own works never reached a broad readership. She characterized herself as "a writer's writer," that is, somebody who influenced other writers, without having a large following of readers herself.

Someone who was clearly influenced by Gertrude Stein, and who himself significantly influenced other writers, is the poet **Ezra Pound** (1885–1972). As one of the most colorful characters of the American modernist circle, Pound strove to revolutionize literature on a large scale. Pound modeled his undertaking on the Italian Renaissance, which was, in an artistic sense, a radical new beginning after the end of the Middle Ages. Pound believed himself to be able to bring about a similar change at the beginning of the twentieth century by reorienting poetry on the past, while at the same time revolutionizing its language. In his later years, this kind of radicalism led him to support Mussolini's fascism in Italy, an allegiance that ultimately resulted in Pound's fall from grace in the literary establishment.

At the beginning of his poetic endeavor, Pound experimented with the Japanese haiku – a short poem with a strictly regulated form and number of syllables, which tries to capture one specific image through a highly focused and condensed mode of expression. Pound was excited by the reductionist approach of this literary genre and, inspired by it, he composed programmatic manifesto-like publications. Following the haiku idea of compressing and condensing an object into an image, Pound founded a lyrical movement called imagism. In his manifesto "A Retrospect" (1918), he postulates: "An 'Image' is ... an ... emotional complex in an instant of time" (4). As with many of his modernist contemporaries, the temporal dimension is the center of Pound's literary contemplation. This concept also lies at the heart of Pound's most famous poem "In a Station of the Metro" (1913):

In a Station of the Metro
The apparition of these faces in the crowd;
Petals on a wet, black bough.

This tercet, based on the Japanese haiku format, reduces the crowd in a subway station to the single image of a wet branch with blossoms. These kinds of seasonal references are typical of the Japanese haiku, which Pound recreates here by using a branch in spring. Pound was equally influenced by the Chinese ideogram, the image-like script in which Japanese haiku were composed. In his unconventional interpretation of the Chinese ideogram as a script akin to pictures, Pound believed it to be an ideal medium for poetry. Pictographic scripts, according to Pound, illustrate the content of what they represent directly, almost unmediated. European alphabetic writing, he argues, lost this immediacy because a major process of abstraction stands between the letters and what they represent. He is convinced that by reducing language to images, or *imagines*, even English poetry can capture elements of the concrete nature of Chinese pictographic writing.

Pound, like his predecessor Walt Whitman, worked throughout his life on his magnum opus, the *Cantos* (1915–1962). Nevertheless, he failed in his attempt to compose a modernist epic that, like the classical or medieval epics of Homer or Dante Alighieri, reflects the knowledge and essence of its culture and period. Pound's complex *Cantos* inevitably remain only glimpses of the fragmented society of the first part of the twentieth century, something he self-consciously comments on when, in the last of his *Cantos*, he writes: "I have brought the great ball of crystal; . . . And I am not a demigod, / I cannot make it cohere" (23.28–29). His epic-like *Cantos* do not bundle the knowledge of an entire era like a multifaceted crystal; on the contrary, his magnum opus disintegrates into fractured perspectives that lack an overall coherence.

Ezra Pound also had a strong, direct influence on **T. S. Eliot** (1888–1965), one of the most successful American modernist authors. Pound, for example, edited and largely rewrote Eliot's major work, the long poem *The Waste Land* (1922). Similarly to Pound's project of reinventing poetry, Eliot, in this text, tries to unite the voices of Renaissance poets, myth, and science. Eliot incorporates, for instance, elements of the grail myth in order to illustrate the psychological wasteland of post-World War I society. In addition to numerous intertextual references, he also uses direct quotes and scholarly footnotes. The poem thereby deliberately blurs the borders between primary and secondary literature. Despite their avant-garde character, the footnotes in *The Waste Land* could also be indebted to the Italian Renaissance. The fourteenth-century writer Giovanni Boccaccio, in his chivalric romance *Teseida* (1340–1341), had already ostensibly used this stylistic feature in order to align his poem with scholarly and religious texts of the period.

In contrast to his mentor Ezra Pound, T. S. Eliot managed to reach a larger audience with his poems, plays, and essays. Until today, Eliot's literary essays, "The Metaphysical Poets" (1921) and "Tradition and the Individual Talent" (1920), are more than just interpretations of literary phenomena from the past. Rather, in an indirect way, they present an insightful self-analysis of the modernist project of renewing literature during the first decades of the twentieth century. Eliot, for example, in his Shakespeare essay "Hamlet and His Problems" (1919), introduces the term "objective correlative," defined as a "set of objects, a situation, a chain of events," that is able to create a "particular emotion" (145). Again, Eliot's primary goal is not to discuss a historical, or hitherto neglected, phenomenon in the works of Shakespeare. On the contrary, the key concept of the essay becomes a theoretical credo, showing parallels to Pound's definition of the "image." Furthermore, the "objective correlative" bears a close resemblance to the conceit of the Metaphysical poets – another of Eliot's interests in his essays, all of which expound positions of a modernist poetics as much as they explain literary phenomena of past historical periods.

Besides Stein, Pound, and Eliot, authors like **Hilda Doolittle** (1886–1961) or **Marianne Moore** (1887–1972) have belatedly been recognized in literary history as major influences on and important voices of American modernist poetry. Their roles in the formation of modernist trends had largely been underestimated. For example, Hilda Doolittle, or H.D., as she refers to herself, was a major force in imagism, a movement that scholars traditionally associated mainly with Ezra Pound. She is most famous for her poems that deal with mythological topics from a feminist perspective, including her epic poem *Helen in Egypt* (1952–1954).

All American modernists discussed so far experienced their literary socialization in Europe, mostly in Paris or London. However, at the same time, a relatively independent group of modernist poets emerged in the United States, among them Wallace Stevens, William Carlos Williams, Robert Frost, and the concrete poet e. e. cummings. While the "European" representatives of American modernism saw the key to a literary reorientation in the cosmopolitan and historical, for those who stayed at home, contemporary local American culture became the starting point of modernist renewal.

This second line of modernist poetry in the United States does not necessarily share the overt experimental or academic finesse of the expatriate poets writing in Europe. For instance, **Robert Frost**'s (1874–1963) "Stopping by Woods on a Snowy Evening," unlike American expatriate texts, is reminiscent of romantic poetry, building on the tension between Nature and the individual self:

> Whose woods these are I think I know
> His house is in the village though;
> He will not see me stopping here
> To watch his woods fill up with snow.

My little horse must think it queer
To stop without a farmhouse near
Between the woods and frozen lake
The darkest evening of the year.

He gives his harness bells a shake
To ask if there is some mistake.
The only other sound's the sweep
Of easy wind and downy flake.

The woods are lovely, dark and deep.
But I have promises to keep,
And miles to go before I sleep,
And miles to go before I sleep.

The wintry idyll of forest, lake, and snowflakes, which the text superficially sketches, camouflages a deeply existentialist question concerning the responsibility of man. The speaker is tied to an implicit pledge, which prompts her or him to fulfill a certain task or promise. Similar to Romantic and transcendentalist poets, some of whom experimented with the narrative perspective of a social outcast or mentally handicapped person, Frost weaves into the poem the unconventional point of view of the horse as judge of the situation. For the horse it seems foolish to risk your life in the freezing woods if you could be in a safer and warmer place in the company of humans. It is hard to say whether the poem expounds a wish for death that eventually gives way to a sense of responsibility and obligation to live. It also has to remain undecided whether the poem expresses the feelings of an overworked Santa Claus, as my young daughter spontaneously claimed when reading the poem for the first time. It is important that Frost utilizes a typical American setting, suspended between wilderness and civilization, in order to explore existentialist questions. In doing so, he positions himself and his poetic project in utter contrast to the cosmopolitan branch of expatriate modernist poetry in the spirit of Pound or Eliot.

Wallace Stevens's (1879–1955) poem "Anecdote of the Jar" (1919) is another example of how autochthonous poets position themselves in contrast to the international strand of modernist American poetry:

> I placed a jar in Tennessee,
> And round it was, upon a hill.
>
> (1–2)

Already the two opening lines seem like a persiflage of John Keats's "Ode on a Grecian Urn" (1819), in which the romantic poet chose a classical Grecian urn as the central object of description. Stevens seems to mock the grand enterprise of the American exile-modernists, Pound and Eliot, who, like Keats in the form of the urn, employ classical cultural traditions with their myths and literary memorials as a starting point for a renewal of poetry. By substituting Keats's classical urn with a mass-produced American glass jar, Stevens also ironically substitutes the classical tradition with an indigenous American material culture. Interestingly, Stevens, with this subliminal allusion to Keats, questions another central aspect of the modernists: their conspicuously propagated renunciation of romanticism and its understanding of literature. Stevens proves two points at the same time. First, he illustrates that a renewal cannot base itself on the classic tradition, especially when this tradition has already been revived several times in different periods, as, for example, in romanticism. Second, in order to achieve this renewal, the project definitely cannot rest on romaticism, the self-declared enemy of the modernist enterprise. So, in a way, Stevens's poem reminds his fellow poets to watch out when seeking reform in poetry by relying on older traditions because, as we can see in romanticism, it has already been done over and over again.

Another writer who overtly toyed with the autochthonous is **William Carlos Williams** (1883–1963), who, in between seeing patients as a physician, composed an abundance of poems, including the famous "The Red Wheelbarrow" (1923):

> so much depends
> upon
>
> a red wheel
> barrow
>
> glazed with rain
> water
>
> beside the white
> chickens.

Again, the poem seems like a parody of the metaphysical conceit, sneering at the "spinning wheel" of Puritan poet Edward Taylor, the object-like metaphor, which Eliot, in the form of the "objective correlative," propagated for modern poetry. Similar to Wallace Stevens, William Carlos Williams uses something profoundly unedifying, something that can be found in front of every American barn. Interestingly enough, Williams's poem achieves the central idea of the poetics of Eliot and Pound, despite, or maybe due to, its ironic tone. The "objective correlative" created by Williams's tableau of objects seems to successfully transport the emotions we associate with American farm-life. At the same time, it seems to fulfill Ezra Pound's definition of the image as an "emotional complex in an instant of time."

Another poet who was similarly interested in the realization of images, although at first sight not necessarily following Pound's imagist spirit, was **e. e. cummings** (1894–1962). The poet eventually turned his back on Europe and worked as a painter and author in the United States. For cummings, poetry is intricately interwoven with the pictorial quality of a text. Following this credo, he indirectly implements Pound's concept of a pictorial language, but puts it into effect in a much more radical fashion. In his concrete poetry, cummings creates a direct correlation between the textual surface and its content. This approach, too, had precursors in the metaphysical poetry of the seventeenth century or the iconic poems of the French surrealists. But cummings goes far beyond the tradition of figuratively arranging letters in order to visually recreate objects. Instead, single linguistic signs, even letters and punctuation marks, become meaningful visual elements, as, for example, in the poem "l(a" (1958), written toward the end of cummings's career:

l(a

le

af

fa

ll

s)

one

l

iness

Reading the poem from the top down, what catches one's eye is that parentheses enclose the words "a leaf falls" within the word "loneliness." We could therefore assume that this is a romantic, maybe even melancholic poem. The topic of loneliness is rendered through a concrete image – Eliot would call it an "objective correlative" – in this case, a single falling leaf. Already the *Iliad* had compared the transience of humans with leaves in the wind. Cummings transports this message also on a visual level, as he visually reenacts the leaf's downward swirl through a number of cunningly arranged textual elements. The opening parenthesis "(" and the later closure ")" illustrate the rotary motion of the leaf when turning from one side to the other. Furthermore, cummings uses the rhetorical figure of chiasmus in the lines "af" and "fa" in order to realize the spiraling movement of the falling leaf even on the smallest linguistic level of the letter. In addition to that, cummings also plays with the typographic ambiguity of letters: "l" can be read as the first-person singular pronoun or the number one. Loneliness becomes "1ness," the result of falling from "ll" or *two*someness, into "1," i.e. solitude. As this example shows, modernist poetry manifests itself in a number of different ways, many of which concern themselves with the pictorial quality of poetical language.

A visual object of a completely different kind lies at the center of **Hart Crane**'s (1899–1932) poem *The Bridge* (1930). In an ode-like manner Crane glorifies America's modern age via an incantation of the bridge between Brooklyn and Manhattan as a masterpiece of modern engineering. Crane, like Eliot, works with classical elements based on Dante and the Italian Renaissance. A ride on the subway, for instance, resembles journeys to the underworld in classical or late medieval epics. The strongest cohesive element of the poem is, however, the concept of the bridge, both as a literary metaphor and a material manifestation of the period's departure into modernity. Preceding the poem, Crane inserts a prayer-like "proem," calling the Brooklyn Bridge a "harp and altar" (46), meaning an object that simultaneously sings the new America and adopts the function of a site of worship of the new America.

Besides these movements of renewal in the genre of poetry, American drama also experienced a major breakthrough around the time of World War I. More precisely, American drama only emerged as a serious genre during that time. In the seventeenth and eighteenth centuries, Puritanism repressed dramatic performances so that American theater, where it existed, heavily depended on European, that is, British imports. When this connection to the unloved mother country was forcefully severed during the War of Independence, American theater of the nineteenth century continued mostly in the form of distorted versions of successful classics. Among the most popular were Shakespeare's plays, often in crude reductions, as well as prose texts, such as *Uncle Tom's Cabin* or "Rip van Winkle," performed as stage adaptations.

It is with **Eugene O'Neill** (1888–1953) that American drama emerged as a serious genre after World War I. O'Neill came from a family of actors whose fame derived from the very practice of adapting novels for the stage. In their case it was the stage version of *The Count of Monte Cristo*, in which Eugene O'Neill's father reached nationwide recognition as an acclaimed actor. Eugene O'Neill's breakthrough as the first major American playwright is closely connected to his play *The Emperor Jones*, which premiered in 1920. The protagonist is Brutus Jones, a runaway African-American convict who gains, and eventually loses, power over an island in the West Indies. Fleeing from his pursuers after a rebellion, Brutus experiences a descent into the abyss of the human psyche. In its interest in the psychology of the unconscious, *The Emperor Jones* is particularly committed to C. G. Jung's theory of archetypes. Brutus Jones's escape becomes a psychological regress in which personal and collective images surface and mentally haunt him. In these hallucinatory sequences, Brutus believes himself to be sent back into nineteenth-century slavery, or to the Africa of his ancestors, thereby gradually delving into his personal unconscious as well as the collective unconscious of his race. O'Neill mainly relies on Jung's theory of archetypes as a possibility for capturing the human condition via collective images.

Besides Jung's depth psychology, O'Neill adopts Friedrich Nietzsche's idea of a mythic Dionysian theater for a cultural renewal of modern drama. These elements are not only at work in *The Emperor Jones*, but also in his other plays, and frequently converge with expressionist features. In some plays, O'Neill uses masks as a link to the cultic quality of Ancient Greek theater, while at the same time experimenting with them as modes of representing the alienated identity of modern man. In *The Emperor Jones*, O'Neill also employs other expressionist elements, like drums gradually getting louder throughout the play, thus mirroring the protagonist's heartbeat, which accelerates parallel to his growing despair.

As one of the first and most important dramas of the twentieth century, *The Emperor Jones* captivates audiences with its unusual choice of an African-American main character. O'Neill certainly manages a dangerous balancing act between racial stereotypes and the renewal of the dramatic genre in the United States. The African-American protagonist Brutus is indeed problematic, as he remains in a stereotypical psychological disposition in which he eagerly trades, when under pressure, civilized rationality for savage superstition. Nevertheless, it is precisely the combination of all these elements, as we will see later, which makes O'Neill's *The Emperor Jones* a typical work of modernism.

At the beginning of the twentieth century, **Susan Glaspell** (1876–1948), in her function as a co-founder of the theater company the Provincetown Players, contributed vitally to establishing drama in the United States. For a long time scholars saw her role mainly in providing a platform for the performances of plays by authors who – like Eugene O'Neill – would later become the big names in American drama. From today's point of view, Glaspell's early plays are especially pertinent to the history of American drama because of their gender-specific concerns. In contrast to her male contemporaries, Glaspell's plays had little or no direct influence on the development of the genre at the time. Only in the second half of the twentieth century did feminist literary criticism recognize Glaspell's achievements as a playwright in her own right, in addition to being a facilitator for dramatic performances of her male colleagues' plays.

Glaspell's one-act play *Trifles* (1916) demonstrates her new and gender-conscious approach. Central to the play, yet at the same time absent throughout the plot, is Minnie, the wife of a homicide victim. Two of Minnie's female friends visiting the crime scene uncover, due to their "female" point of view, the real background and motive for the crime. In contrast to the men on the scene, these two women are able to "read" certain inconsistencies in the house as evidence for the husband's oppression of Minnie, as well as evidence testifying to the fact that Minnie killed her husband. While the men search only the "male" domains of the house, such as the toolshed or the bedroom, the women inspect the kitchen, discovering important leads concerning the crime and its motive. The first hint is a half-finished quilt, unexpectedly showing untidy seams, which do not fit into the wife's otherwise perfect work. Their second observation is a dead canary in the wife's sewing box. As it turns out, the husband strangled the canary, and the wife, identifying with the caged bird, murdered her husband in the same way. At the end of the play, the two women remove all evidence that would point to Minnie as the murderer and keep their discovery to themselves.

In the play, Glaspell toys with the concept of "text," as texture or textile, in the form of the "telltale" quilt. Female "readers" of the quilt interpret the strands of narrative that the seams spell out differently than the professional male investigators. Glaspell's play becomes an allegory of gender-specific reading and perception processes – similar to Gilman's "The Yellow Wallpaper," with its double meaning of "paper," as both wallpaper and text. Despite these innovative and intriguing aspects of the play, Glaspell shares with Gilman the fate of belated recognition, since both authors had to wait for more than half a century to be granted their rightful place beside male authors in the American literary canon.

Besides Glaspell and O'Neill, **Elmar Rice** (1892–1967) is one of the three great reformers of American theater after World War I. Especially his play *The Adding Machine* (1923) marks the beginning of expressionist theater in the United States. The main character of the play is Mr. Zero, who, after twenty-five years of good work, is made redundant when the company replaces him by an adding machine. Beside himself with rage, Mr. Zero kills his boss, is sentenced to death, and, in the afterlife, gets reemployed on the Elysian Fields where he is forced to operate an adding machine until he is made redundant again so that his soul can be sent back to earth in order to serve in a new body.

The Adding Machine, similar to a number of texts in the American literary tradition, displays and problematizes a Puritan work ethic. In order to achieve this critique, Rice uses expressionist elements in stage design, such as specific lighting, and renders his characters with mask-like features. In its crude reduction of the figures to stereotypical character traits, the play seems to draw on mask-like elements from ancient drama and medieval allegorizations of human virtues and vices. With its nihilistic plot, its seemingly senseless direction, and its flat characters, *The Adding Machine*, already in the 1920s, anticipates aspects of the theater of the absurd in the middle and the second half of the century. On the other hand, the socioeconomic subject matter of the play also paves the way for the socialist drama of the 1930s, focusing on the role of the worker as well as unjust modes of production.

As we have already seen with Eugene O'Neill and Gertrude Stein, modernism at the beginning of the twentieth century experimented with African culture, which, due to its seeming naturalness and unspoiled primitivism, served as a role model for innovation and renewal. It inspired painters like Pablo Picasso, who in turn influenced the visual arts as well as the literature of the period. It is thus not surprising that Gertrude Stein, as a literary proponent of cubism and catalyst figure of American modernism, chose an African-American protagonist for her prose text "Melanctha." In a similar move, Eugene O'Neill, the reformer and founder of American drama, centered his play around the black figure of Brutus Jones.

Parallel to nonblack authors, borrowing from African culture in the 1920s, a strong strand of African-American self-expression evolved in an unprecedented way around the same time. This flare of artistic black confidence, also called the "Harlem Renaissance," continues in literature the tradition of African-American intellectuals around the turn of the century. The groundbreaking *The Souls of Black Folk* (1903) by the sociologist **W. E. B. Du Bois** (1868–1963), together with **Booker T. Washington**'s (1856–1915) works, were among the first African-American theoretical views on race relations. Drawing on this climate of African-American self-expression in the social sciences, authors like **Langston Hughes** (1902–1967) emerged as the most important representatives of the Harlem Renaissance in the 1920s. Hughes's poems, together with the works of other African-American poets, appeared in **Alain Locke**'s (1885–1954) landmark verse anthology *The New Negro* (1925).

Especially during the interwar period, the fiction of female African-American authors, such as **Zora Neale Hurston** (1891–1960) in *Their Eyes Were Watching God* (1937), captivated audiences with self-confident female protagonists. Similarly, **Nella Larsen**'s (1891–1964) novel *Passing* (1929) focuses on a woman protagonist, taking a female approach to the topic of racial passing by stripping the theme of the rather stereotypical and sentimental treatment by white authors in nineteenth-century melodrama. The notion of African Americans passing for whites also made its way into the cinema of the first half of the twentieth century with films such as *Imitation of Life* (1934). It is also important to note that especially in the 1920s and 1930s, an independent African-American cinema evolved. Black directors, such as the famous **Oscar Micheaux** (1884–1951), made films with an all-black cast for a specifically black audience. During the Great Depression and the race riots at the beginning of the 1930s, the Harlem Renaissance lost momentum, finding a continuation in somewhat different, more fragmented, African-American voices in the second half of the twentieth century.

Of course, the city of New York as a place for modernist literary renewal was not limited to Harlem. Starting around the turn of the century, with realists like Theodore Dreiser, the metropolis continued to serve as a projection screen for diverse literary agendas into the 1920s and 1930s. Those modernists who, unlike Eliot and Pound, sought cultural renewal in America, stylized the uniqueness of New York for their specific concerns.

Especially the novels of the Jazz Age perpetuated the realist and naturalist traditions of the urban novel. **F. Scott Fitzgerald**'s (1896–1940) *The Great Gatsby* (1925) becomes the epitome of the roaring twenties with their exuberant parties and excesses – a decadent lifestyle that Scott and his wife Zelda shared with the protagonists of their novels, thanks to Fitzgerald's early success as a writer. Even though stylistically less experimental than many other modernist novels, *The Great Gatsby* draws in readers through its choice of narrative perspective. The events around the mysterious, rich social climber Gatsby are told from the point of view of a minor character of the novel. The choice of Nick Carraway as the narrator of the events is reminiscent of Melville's *Moby Dick*, in which the sailor Ishmael, from the periphery, characterizes the enigmatic Captain Ahab. In English literature of the premodern period, Joseph Conrad's (1857–1924) novella *Heart of Darkness* (1902) also uses this narrative technique in order to mystify the character of the ivory trader and monstrous colonist Kurtz.

The plot of Fitzgerald's novel revolves around the enigmatic Gatsby, who gained his newly accumulated wealth under mysterious circumstances. The story is fueled by an affair between Gatsby and the love of his youth, Daisy, now married to the rich but boring Tom

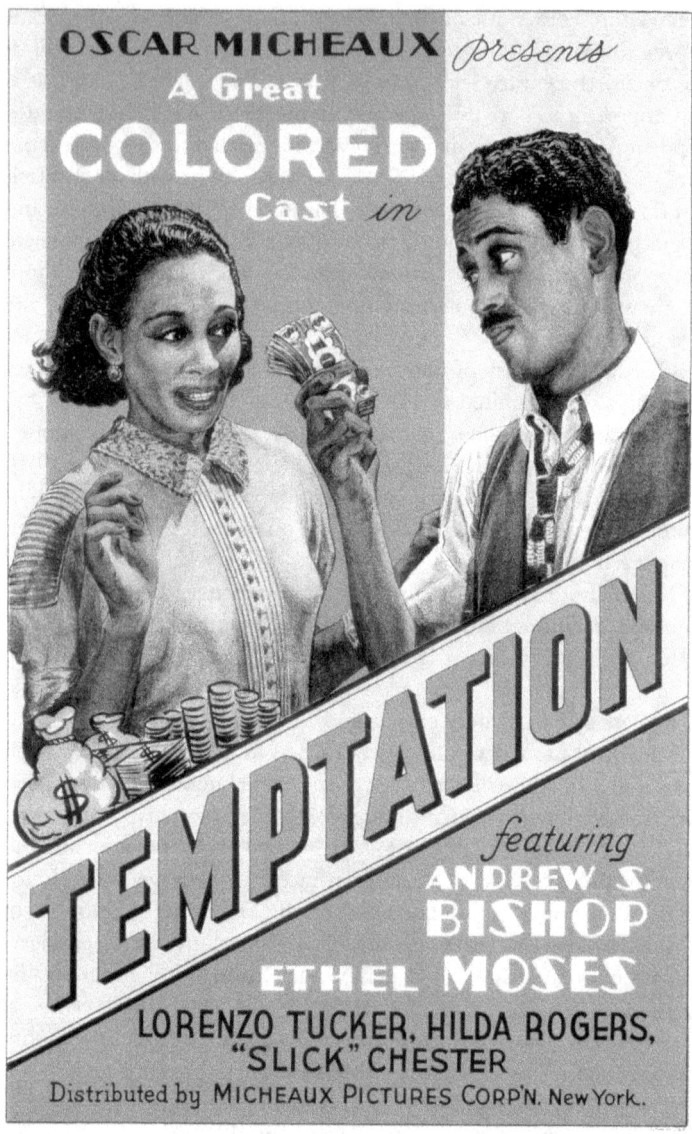

Figure 7.2 Movie poster for *Temptation* (1936), directed by Oscar Micheaux.

Buchanan. One day, while driving Gatsby's car, Daisy kills a woman in a traffic accident. Panic-stricken, Daisy flees the scene and lets Gatsby heroically take the blame for the accident as well as the death of the woman. Mistaking Gatsby for the responsible driver in the accident, the husband of the victim kills Gatsby in revenge. Despite all of this, Daisy resumes her position in her marriage, finding comfort in the security of her husband's money, which, from the beginning, had formed the basis of their relationship. *The Great Gatsby* is a genre picture of the American society of the Jazz Age in the 1920s before the Great Depression. At the same time, however, it glorifies the American dream of the "self-made man," a figure that will evolve as a central character of the new social novel in the decades to come.

While Fitzgerald's document of the Jazz Age does not show any clearly identifiable political trajectory, **John Dos Passos**'s (1896–1970) trilogy *U.S.A.* is much more unambiguous in this respect. His novels, *The 42nd Parallel* (1930), *1919* (1932), and *The Big Money* (1936), represent the concerns of the "red thirties" after the Great Depression, marked by left-wing literary politicking, as well as toying with socialism and communist ideas. The trilogy covers a time frame of about thirty years, from the turn of the century to the early 1930s. Besides numerous fictional characters who appear in a loose network throughout the novels, Dos Passos weaves into the picture real-life figures from politics, economics, and the arts. For instance, biographical information on Henry Ford, Isadora Duncan, and Woodrow Wilson at times interrupts the plot that is otherwise based on fictional characters. Besides this particular narrative technique, Dos Passos's novels make collage-like use of newspaper headlines, song lyrics, or political speeches that appear in an aphoristic manner at the beginning of chapters. Referred to as "newsreels" by Dos Passos, they were supposed to achieve a similar effect on the audiences as the newsreels that preceded movie shows in the cinema of the time. Specific to the trilogy are the "camera-eye" passages, which, interspersed throughout the novels, document the subjective point of view of an adolescent young man in the form of a stream-of-consciousness narration.

This exuberant play with unconventional points of view already announced itself in the choice of a minor character in Fitzgerald's *The Great Gatsby* and reaches its climax in the high modernism of Dos Passos as well as in the fiction of the Southern author **William**

Faulkner (1897–1962). In the novel *The Sound and the Fury* (1929), Faulkner uses four people, who, from four different points of view, throw light on four different time frames in the life of a Southern family. The most outstanding and, for the reader, most demanding part is the so-called "Benjy-section," which is told from the point of view of Benjy, the youngest member of the family, who is mentally challenged – hence the title of the novel, which is part of a Shakespeare verse from *Macbeth*: "a tale / Told by an idiot, full of sound and fury" (5.5.26–27).

When going through the Benjy-section of the novel, the reader inevitably has to assume the role of a detective, as Benjy perceives the world in a highly unconventional way. This special mode of perception passes on information in an unfiltered and unexplained manner, as the following passage illustrates. As in hundreds of other instances, the reader has to decipher one of Benjy's observations, trying to solve the question of what it actually is that Benjy witnesses in his limited perceptive mode: "It was red, flapping on the pasture. . . . I held to the fence. . . . Maybe we can find one of they balls"(11–12). Benjy is observing a game of golf, a game of which he knows neither the rules nor its overall purpose. He simply registers the red flags and the white balls. Faulkner, in using the mentally challenged Benjy, positions himself in the long tradition of authors, going back to Mark Twain, who also relied on unconventional narrators. Furthermore, Faulkner continues his experiments in realism and naturalism, which confronted the reader directly with a character's perception of his or her external reality. As different as Faulkner's and Henry James's texts are in their choice of subject matter, realism and modernism become very similar in trying to depict perception or, in Faulkner's case, the extreme alienation of perception. Reading the Benjy-section leads to a defamiliarization effect – a kind of constant epiphany – answering the question of how perception works in general. The point of view of Faulkner's "idiot" becomes necessary in order to spell out for the reader the fundamental processes at work in perception and in the formation of consciousness as such.

Also in other texts, especially in the novel *As I Lay Dying* (1930), Faulkner experiments with narrative techniques when he spins together fifty-nine monologues by seven different family members into a polyphonic plot circling around a funeral procession. Like the majority of his texts, it is set in the fictional Yoknapatawpha County, which Faulkner stylizes as an imaginary manifestation of the American South. Although Faulkner had already written his major works in the 1920s, he achieved full recognition and literary success only after the end of World War II, around the time he was awarded the Nobel Prize for Literature.

Modernist literature does not have to exhibit the conspicuous complexity of Faulkner's texts. On the contrary, it can be of an almost primitive simplicity, as, for example, the fiction of **Ernest Hemingway** (1898–1961). Despite winning the Nobel Prize for Literature and gaining international recognition by a broad mass of readers, the literary judgment about Hemingway has never been homogenous. A large part of Hemingway's popularity can certainly be attributed to his topics, which addressed concerns of the time, such as war experience and postwar trauma. A volunteer and wounded paramedic during the Spanish Civil War, Hemingway, in the majority of his works, returns to archetypal situations of crisis which his protagonists try to resolve. His heroes are the *toreros* of Spanish bullfighting, as in *The Sun Also Rises* (1926), or lonesome fighters who combat elemental forces, like the fisherman in *The Old Man and the Sea* (1951). This choice of topics, and the fact that women hardly ever play a role in his novels, made Hemingway an easy and justified target for feminist literary criticism in the second half of the twentieth century. On the other hand, exactly these choices of protagonists singled Hemingway out as a preferred object for masculinity studies toward the end of the twentieth century.

Hemingway's simple language and narrative technique seems, at least at first glance, to regress stylistically when compared to the other modernist innovators of fiction. No matter how we react to or evaluate his mode of storytelling, Hemingway consciously chose simple narrative structures and simple diction, a style that in several aspects borrowed from the medium of film. If we take a closer look at a randomly picked passage from a Hemingway text, for example, the beginning of the short story "The Killers" (1927), it becomes clear that he renders the scene as if viewed through a film camera, unnoticed and without commentary:

> The door of Henry's lunch-room opened and two men came in. They sat down at the counter.

> 'What's yours?' George asked them.
>
> 'I don't know,' one of the men said. 'What do you want to eat, Al?'
>
> 'I don't know,' said Al. 'I don't know what I want to eat.'
>
> Outside it was getting dark. The street-light came on outside the window. The two men at the counter read the menu. From the other end of the counter Nick Adams watched them. He had been talking to George when they came in.
>
> (378)

The narrator disappears almost completely, dialogue takes over, and the reader is seemingly left alone with the utterances of the characters. Again, this is a technique that finds its main premise in concepts of the realist novel in the mode of Henry James. Hemingway's texts thereby obtain something immediate, almost drama-like. Analyses by the Swiss scholar Max Nänny have impressively shown that the simple surface of Hemingway's texts can at times hide a very complex deep structure. In some cases, Hemingway – similar to Gertrude Stein – uses repetitive, mirroring elements on a syntactical level, generating a diverse network of brace-like interlacing.

John Steinbeck (1902–1968), too, returned in his novels to seemingly traditional forms of narration. Committed to the ideas of the "red thirties," his most important novel *The Grapes of Wrath* (1939) tells the story of the financially troubled Joad family. After crop failures due to soil erosion, they leave their land in Oklahoma in an attempt to try their luck in California. Their journey to the alleged Golden West turns into a reversal of the American Dream, ending in disillusionment and a situation that severely threatens the family's very survival. Together with its filmic adaptation, Steinbeck's novel became a classic about the dark side of the American Dream, questioning its principle that hard work will eventually be rewarded with success – wishful thinking that had been dominating American self-understanding from colonial times onward.

Besides the novel, the newly emerging genre of drama took up sociopolitical and socioeconomic questions as well. Among the social dramas of the 1930s, **Clifford Odets**'s (1906–1963) *Waiting for Lefty* (1935) stands out in a number of ways. In addition to the political agenda the play foregrounds, by using a planned labor strike by taxi drivers for its plot, it breaks new ground in experimenting with the illusion of a self-contained world onstage. Integrating the theater audience into the play by planting actors among the theatergoers and eventually letting them react to the comments made by actors onstage seemingly dissolves the barriers that separate theater from real life. Feminist plays also emerged in this period, including **Lillian Hellman**'s (1905–1984) *The Children's Hour* (1934) about the rumors around an alleged lesbian relationship of two teachers and their stigmatization by society.

Before the theater of the absurd and postmodern theater developed during the second half of the twentieth century, midcentury drama seemed, once again, to become aware of its modernist or even realist roots. Part of this development are plays like **Thornton Wilder**'s (1897–1975) *Our Town* (1937), which depicts everyday life in small-town America and is set in two acts in the years 1901 and 1913. A noteworthy feature of the play is that a "stage director" introduces and comments on both acts. With these frame narratives Wilder manages, in a move reminiscent of Brecht's alienation effect, to deliberately break the illusion of the theatrical space as a self-contained world.

Tennessee Williams (1911–1983) uses a similar technique in his psychological drama classic *The Glass Menagerie* (1944) by implementing a narrator of a frame story. The narrator Tom "remembers" scenes from the past about his physically handicapped sister Laura, whose isolation from her surroundings is symbolized by a collection of glass animals – hence the title *The Glass Menagerie*. The family's world of make-believe shatters during one of their mother's arranged visits, as Laura's childhood sweetheart unintentionally breaks a glass unicorn, kisses her, and then tells her of his engagement to another woman.

In a similar vein, Williams's psychodrama *A Streetcar Named Desire* (1947) is structured around issues of family relations and sexuality, this time centering on an extensive visit of the aging Blanche Du Bois at her sister's place in New Orleans. The interaction with her macho brother-in-law, Stanley Kowalski – played by young Marlon Brando in a successful film adaptation – confronts Blanche with her inglorious, dishonest love life. Suffering from severe mental instability, and after being raped by Stanley, she is "diagnosed" with a nervous breakdown and institutionalized.

Besides Thornton Wilder and Tennessee Williams, **Arthur Miller** (1915–2005) counts as the third great dramatist of late modernism. Miller's *Death of a Salesman* (1949) exemplifies the economic pressure to succeed in the American middle class by focusing on the character of the 60-year-old salesman Willy Loman. Using a stream-of-consciousness technique with extensive flashbacks to his earlier life, Miller portrays Willy's futile struggle as an aging breadwinner in a success-oriented society. His disillusionment eventually gives way to desperation when Willy ends his life in suicide, disguised as a car crash in order to make sure his family receives money from his life insurance. In his death Willy paradoxically manages to provide financial support for his family, a goal he had failed to reach in his life. While being unable to fulfill the harsh requirements of the capitalist system in life, in his martyr-like death he conforms to the system after all.

Equally linked to the American Dream in the widest sense of the term is Miller's *The Crucible* (1953), a play set in Puritan New England during the Salem witchcraft trials, one of the darkest chapters of American colonial history. In his play, Miller uses the persecution of innocent people in the late seventeenth century only as a pretense to hint at the hunt for alleged communists in the McCarthy era of the 1950s. Witch-hunting for Miller becomes a parable of mass hysteria, identical to the activism kindled by the conservative United States senator Joseph McCarthy after World War II. Alleged communists – similar to seventeenth-century witches – were put on trial in order to serve as scapegoats onto which the public rage of the Cold War era could easily unload itself.

8 Postmodernism

The transition from modernism to postmodernism in the late 1950s also brought about a paradigmatic change in drama, similar to the groundbreaking shifts in fiction, which we will discuss later. The term postmodernism refers to a movement in literary and cultural history in the second half of the twentieth century which takes up issues that were treated by modernism – for example, innovative narrative techniques and plot patterns – dealing with them in an academic, often self-reflexive or metafictional way. **Edward Albee**'s (1928–) adaptation of the theater of the absurd for an American context, especially in *The Zoo Story* (1958), becomes a milestone of postmodern theater. The play, similar to Samuel Beckett's *Waiting for Godot*, is rendered in real time on a park bench, in this case in New York's Central Park. Jerry, an alienated and unhappy homosexual, meets the assimilated middle-class representative Peter, whom he engages in a conversation. Eventually, Jerry attacks Peter with a knife, deliberately dropping it in order for Peter to self-reflexively pick it up and use it in his defense. Jerry takes advantage of the situation and hurls himself at the knife in Peter's hand to end his own life. Too late Peter realizes Jerry's plan to set him up as a figure in an orchestrated suicide in which Peter had to take on the role of the societal force that was responsible for Jerry's misery and eventually also for his death. Confused by this recognition and his involuntary role in the "drama," Peter hurriedly flees from the scene in order not to be held accountable for the deed.

Similarly absurd is the plot of Albee's best-known play, *Who's Afraid of Virginia Woolf?* (1962), which focuses on a married couple at a dinner party. The dialogue between the two, again and again, returns to the topic of their son, a figure who, despite their heated arguments, seems to be a common focal point for the couple. In the end, however, we learn that the child is solely an invention of their imagination. It becomes clear that with uncovering this "life lie" – a concept Albee borrowed from Henrik Ibsen's naturalist dramas – their lives fall apart and their common purpose in life disintegrates into despair.

Albee is, of course, not the only playwright to employ these concepts, which are typical of the theater of the absurd. Another famous example is the play *Dutchman* (1964) by the African-American author **LeRoi Jones** (1934–), who later changes his "slave name" to **Amiri Baraka**. *Dutchman* substitutes the park bench in Albee's *Zoo Story* with a seat in the New York City Subway. Here, the seductive white Lula approaches the young African American Clay, engaging him in a flirtatious conversation. As their encounter proceeds, Lula then insults Clay, continuously mocking him for his assimilated lifestyle, which, according to her, does not comply with his racial identity. In the end, she stabs him in front of all the other passengers, who do nothing to stop her. The play ends with Lula turning toward another well-dressed young African American, her next victim. Baraka's play discusses the two central poles of African-American self-definition in the 1960s. On the one hand, there is Martin Luther King's endeavor for assimilation, and on the other hand, Malcolm X's radical separation policy. *Dutchman* clearly takes the position of the latter, promoting an independent African-American culture, not striving for assimilation or integration as its main goal, but advocating segregation as a celebration of difference and self-realization instead.

An earlier African-American play, **Lorraine Hansberry**'s (1930–1965) *A Raisin in the Sun* (1959), also approaches this problem, but from a slightly different angle. Discussing the mobbing of an African-American widow and her grown-up children by white neighbors, the question of integration is coupled with feminist issues about the role of women in African-American families. The 1961 movie version, with young Sidney Poitier in the leading male role, contributed greatly to the popularity of Hansberry's play.

In the second half of the twentieth century, American drama increased its existing affinity to film even more. In the 1970s and 1980s, **David Mamet** (1947–) achieved a broad impact with plays such as *Sexual Perversity in Chicago* (1974) and *Glengarry Glen Ross* (1984), not least because of successful filmic adaptations. *Glengarry Glen Ross*, which is set in the realtor business, appears like an updated version of Arthur Miller's *Death of a Salesman*, as the plot centers around a number of middle-class sales reps struggling to survive in a highly competitive business environment. Pressured from above by their corporate office, the sales reps see their daily routines turned into sales competitions, threatening those who do not perform best to lose their jobs and material bases of existence. The performances by a high-caliber cast in the film version of Mamet's play resulted in the nomination of Al Pacino for an Academy Award and a Golden Globe as supporting actor.

The dramatist, scriptwriter, director, and actor **Sam Shepard** (1943–) maintains a similarly close relationship to film. Early in his career, Shepard created a number of screenplays for films like Michelangelo Antonioni's *Zabriskie Point* (1970), Wim Wender's *Paris, Texas* (1984), and Robert Altman's *Fool for Love* (1985), and wrote successful plays like *True West* (1980). He has also appeared as an actor in major releases, such as *The Pelican Brief* (1993) and *The Pledge* (2001).

Like drama's ventures into new modes of expression under the auspices of film and television, the poetry of the postwar era shows a general atmosphere of departure and protest. A radical renewal of American poetry takes place with the Beat Generation in the 1950s. In the same spirit as **Jack Kerouac** (1922–1969), who captures the sense of departure of the rebellious 1950s in his drug-imbued "road novel" *On the Road* (1951), **Lawrence Ferlinghetti** (1919–) and **Allen Ginsberg** (1926–1997) try to express the spirit of the age in their poetry. Ginsberg, in particular, saw himself in the tradition of the sexual poetry of Walt Whitman, deliberately provoking the establishment with direct homosexual subject matter. In accordance with the spirit of the Beat Generation, Ginsberg amalgamates open protest, drug consumption, and overt sexuality into an explosive mixture, as already hinted at by the opening verses of his most controversial poem "Howl" (1956):

> I saw the best minds of my generation destroyed by
> madness, starving hysterical naked,
> dragging themselves through the negro streets at dawn
> looking for an angry fix,

> angelheaded hipsters burning for the ancient heavenly
>> connection to the starry dynamo in the machinery
>> of night.
>
>> (1–3)

Descriptions of homosexuality and homosexual practices in "Howl," such as "who let themselves be fucked in the ass" (36), confronted Lawrence Ferlinghetti's publishing company with a lawsuit for spreading obscenities, thereby causing a controversy that went far beyond the boundaries of literary circles. In many respects, the unconventional life and writing styles of the beatniks, governed by sexuality and drugs, had a significant influence on the emancipatory counterculture of the 1960s at large.

Less provoking were the poetic works of the so-called Black Mountain School with **Denise Levertov** (1923–1997), **Charles Olson** (1910–1970), and **Robert Creeley** (1926–2005). Charles Olson, in his essay "Projective Verse" (1950), called for an "open field" of composition in order to replace traditional closed poetic forms. Breath – and not rhyme and meter – should reflect the content of the poem and therefore be a poet's central concern. A poem's form needs to be based on the line, and each line should be a unit of breath and of utterance. Olson's essay, which deliberately places itself in the tradition of Ezra Pound's programmatic writing, assumed the status of a manifesto for the Black Mountain poets. Some proponents of this other strand of American post-World War II poetry can seem rather academic and theoretical, as, for example, **John Ashberry**'s (1927–) poem *Self-Portrait in a Convex Mirror* (1975). Ashberry discusses postmodern theoretical concerns of representation by using as his object of description the unconventional Renaissance self-portrait of the painter Parmigianino, a picture showing the painter distorted in a convex mirror.

The transition from modernism to postmodernism is blurry not only in poetry and drama, but also in fiction. In the 1950s, **Ralph Ellison** (1914–1994) contributed to the renewal of the genre with his African-American novel *Invisible Man* (1953). Its first-person narrator and protagonist sits in an underground room lit by 1,361 light bulbs, where, forgotten by the rest of the world, he tells his life story as an intelligent black man in white America during the first half of the twentieth

Postmodernism 97

Figure 8.1 Self-portrait in a convex mirror (*c*.1523–1524) by Parmigianino.

century. The setting and the narrative perspective are reminiscent of Fyodor Dostoyevsky's short novel *Notes from Underground* (1864). The unfolding story of the African-American narrator covers his graduation at the top of his class from a high school in the Deep South, his student years at a black college, his trade union activities as a factory worker in New York, and his participation in the Harlem riots. The protagonist discovers that blacks, although despised by and invisible for white American culture – thus the title *Invisible Man* – are essential for the self-definition of white identity. In a central passage of the novel, the protagonist, while working in a paint factory, realizes that, for the production of a can of pure white paint, ten drops of black paint have to be added to achieve the true effect of white. With the end of his life story the narrative comes full circle, returning to the underground room, the place where this long flashback about his life story commenced. Ralph Ellison, in addition to his contributions to the development of the twentieth-century novel, is one of the major voices advocating a new search for identity among marginalized ethnic groups.

Sylvia Plath's (1932–1963) texts are concerned with identity from a gender-oriented perspective. In the *roman à clef The Bell Jar* (1963), Plath negotiates her own psychic breakdown, which, one month after the publication of her novel, led her to commit suicide. The book tells the story of the psychologically troubled first-person narrator Ester Greenwood. The title and central metaphor of the novel is a bell jar under which Esther sees herself trapped in her depression. Plath's novel is reminiscent of Charlotte Perkins Gilman's representation of mental illness before the background of a male-dominated medical environment.

In the second half of the twentieth century, female voices in fiction keep growing stronger, including authors such as **Flannery O'Connor** (1925–1964), whose works contain grotesque elements that are connected to the American South. Her short story "A Good Man Is Hard to Find" (1953) exhibits some typical features of Connor's style, a style that is often referred to as "Southern Gothic." During a stop on a car trip, a family falls into the hands of a gang of runaway prisoners led by The Misfit. After seeing her entire family killed by the outlaws, the grandmother engages in a futile attempt to save herself by gradually bonding with The Misfit, which, however, does not prevent The Misfit from shooting the grandmother in cold blood when she tries to touch him. Typical of O'Connor's fiction are moments of crisis in which a person experiences a deep insight. O'Connor borrows these "moments of epiphany" from James Joyce, adapting them in her own way for her often religiously motivated texts. The absurd violence in "A Good Man Is Hard to Find" seems to anticipate the phantasmagoric aesthetics of violence in recent film, including Quentin Tarantino's *Pulp Fiction* (1994) and *Inglourious Basterds* (2009).

Besides violence, coming-of-age is another major topic in texts of mid-twentieth-century authors, including **Carson McCullers**'s (1917–1967) *The Member of the Wedding* (1946), which is told from the point of view of the troubled 12-year-old Frankie, a tomboy imagining a future with her brother and his bride. The genre is epitomized by **J. D. Salinger**'s (1919–2010) *The Catcher in the Rye* (1951), one of the best-selling novels of the twentieth century. Providing insight into the psyche of the adolescent Holden Caulfield, the book apparently expressed and reflected the wishes, fears, and concerns of generations of teenage readers in the post-World War II era. With a direct reference to first-person narratives in the style of Charles Dickens's *David Copperfield*, Holden recounts his experiences while wandering around Manhattan for three days after having been expelled from high school. His futile search for human closeness ends in a nervous breakdown and subsequent psychiatric treatment.

Salinger also deals with psychological problems of the postwar generation in his short stories. In "A Perfect Day for Bananafish" (1948), the main character Seymour is troubled by imagined problems, such as a tattoo on his leg which he wants to hide from other beachgoers. While swimming, he tells a little girl the story of the bananafish in an underwater cave, that stuffs itself so much with food that it is unable to escape through the narrow cave opening and dies there. After this encounter Seymour goes to his hotel room, sits on the bed next to his sleeping wife, and commits suicide by shooting himself in the head. The short story anticipates, in the genre of fiction, elements of the theater of the absurd, aspects that helped Salinger to gain recognition as a celebrated author. At the same time, he completely withdrew from society for the rest of his career, no longer willing to disclose any information about himself to the public. Toward the end of his life this obsession became so strong that he even sued his own daughter for publishing a book about him.

Although Salinger's texts exhibit features of the absurd, he cannot be counted in the inner circle of American postmodern authors. Closer to the idea of postmodernism, a movement that grew out of modernism's concern with finding a new voice in all fields of literature, is **Vladimir Nabokov** (1899–1977). Born in Russia, Nabokov emigrated to the United States, writing his major works in English, all of which are characterized by typically postmodern features, such as academic self-referencing and literary defamiliarization. His novel *Pale Fire* (1962), for example, uses the structure of a text edition of a 999-line poem by the fictional author John Shade, edited and commented on by the fictional editor Charles Kinbote. In doing so, Nabokov, like

T. S. Eliot in his poem *The Waste Land*, but on a much broader scale, moves back and forth between primary and secondary literature. However, while modernist literature had used elements of defamiliarization less ostensively, postmodernism foregrounds them in an exaggerated, almost academic way.

Nabokov's greatest success was his novel *Lolita* (1955), which describes, from a first-person perspective, the pathological love relationship between the aging university professor Humbert Humbert and his initially 12-year-old stepdaughter Dolores. Humbert's pedophile inclination, caused by an unfulfilled and psychologically unresolved teenage love, prompts the first-person narrator to engage in a sexual relationship with his underage stepdaughter. After the death of the teenager's mother, under the pretext of a father-daughter relationship, he and Dolores tour the United States for more than two years. Eventually, Dolores elopes with a book editor who had been following Humbert for some time. Years later, when Humbert eventually finds Dolores, pregnant by another lover, he is no longer interested in the now grown-up woman, but only wants her to disclose the whereabouts of the editor. When Dolores reveals the identity of her former abductor, Humbert seeks out the editor and kills him in revenge.

Lolita has numerous self-reflexive or metafictional elements that will become staples of postmodernist fiction: Humbert Humbert is a literature professor, the helper in Dolores's flight is a book editor, and Humbert's narrative, which he discloses to an inmate after the murder, is edited by a fictitious editor. Nabokov's *Lolita* was not an immediate success. In fact, only via its European reception did the scandalous novel eventually receive wide recognition in the United States. Especially the detailed inside perspective of the pedophile first-person narrator made American publishers at first shy away from releasing the novel for the US market.

Nabokov was a major influence on subsequent American fiction writers, for example, **Thomas Pynchon** (1937–), who incorporated elements of his teacher but also pursued idiosyncratic goals. Pynchon shares with his contemporary J. D. Salinger an extreme concern for privacy when it comes to disclosing any kind of personal information. However, Pynchon is much more playful and self-conscious about his secrecy. His only known public "appearances" are as a cartoon character

Figure 8.2 Thomas Pynchon's 2004 appearance in *The Simpsons* (season 15, episode 10).

in episodes of *The Simpsons* in which he lends his authentic voice to a cartoon figure with a paper bag over his head.

Pynchon's novels and short stories, with their self-referential and metafictional traits, as well as their seemingly paradoxical plots, are prime examples of postmodernist narratives, which resist one-dimensional interpretations or explanations. In *The Crying of Lot 49* (1966) the protagonist Oedipa Maas is confronted with a mysterious eighteenth-century underground organization. Cryptic signs spread around town testify to its existence. After meeting with a number of eccentric characters, Oedipa hopes to find explanations about the organization in a stamp collection that is to be auctioned. In its enigmatic and paradoxical plot, Pynchon's fiction anticipates films and television series of the late twentieth century, for example, David Lynch's *Twin Peaks* (1990–1991).

Raymond Federman (1928–2009) practiced a very different, often playful variant of postmodern American fiction. In his first novel *Double or Nothing* (1971), he experimented with typographical features in a manner reminiscent of conventions in concrete poetry. As a French Jew, Federman escaped death only by a hair's breadth. His mother hid the little boy in a closet when the Nazis deported her and the rest of the family to a concentration camp, from which none of them returned. In his novels, including *The Voice in the Closet* (1979), despite their playfulness, Federman kept coming back to this primordial closet scene that so decisively shaped his life.

We find another form of war experience running through American literary history in novels about coming to terms with the traumas of soldiers during World War II, the Korean War, or the Vietnam War. **Kurt Vonnegut**'s (1922–2007) *Slaughterhouse-Five* (1969) is not only a good example for postmodernist fiction trying to find a voice for describing the atrocities of war, but also an example of how these experiences shaped the stylistic features of postmodernism as such. Vonnegut, who survived the bombardment of Dresden as a young American soldier, an event in which over 200,000 civilians were killed, seeks a voice to express these events in his novel. He employs, or even develops, a postmodern narrative structure in which the autobiographically imbued figure of Billy Pilgrim becomes the focal point of a multiperspectival story. The story fragments comprise Billy's experiences as a young soldier during the Dresden bombardment, episodes from his life before and after the war, as well as a science-fiction-like level in which Billy is abducted by extraterrestrials to the faraway planet Tralfamadore and exhibited naked in a zoo. The juxtaposition of these perspectives creates an intriguing impression of the omnipresence of the traumatic war experiences, transgressing time and space in the mind of the shell-shocked protagonist.

Vonnegut skillfully plays with the concept of simultaneity of these different plot levels, partly borrowing from modernist narrative strategies, by experimenting with fragmentation and multiperspectival cubist representational practices. In a metafictional passage of the novel, Vonnegut self-reflexively draws attention to his technique, while seemingly explaining the alien literature and writing practice of the Tralfamadorians. Their literature consists of a large number of little fragments, which they do not read in a linear or sequential way. Rather, they take them in as a whole: "when seen all at once, they produce an image of life that is beautiful and surprising and deep. . . . marvelous moments seen all at one time" (71). Vonnegut thus suggests that the fragmentary vignettes in his novel, encompassing present, memory, and imagination of the traumatized protagonist, should also be seen, or better read, as one simultaneous projection.

Vonnegut positioned his novel in the long tradition of American war fiction, which, beginning with Stephen Crane's *The Red Badge of Courage*, managed to come to terms with war-induced trauma in American history. However, some novels perform this task through satire, such as **Joseph Heller**'s (1923–1999) novel *Catch-22* (1961), which lays bare the economically motivated scheming of the military on a fictitious World War II military base in the Mediterranean. In a similar vein, popular culture in the aftermath of the Vietnam War used the Korean War as the setting for the TV comedy series *M*A*S*H* (1972–1983).

Among the "academic" proponents of American postmodernist fiction are **William Gass** (1924–), who, in the essay "Philosophy and the Form of Fiction" (1970), coined the term "metafiction" – a term to become almost synonymous with postmodernism. It denotes fiction about fiction, meaning self-reflexive literary texts that focus on their own literary elements, such as language, narrative, or plot structure. Also the novelist **John Barth** (1930–) contributed theoretical essays to the literary landscape in an attempt to define and shape American postmodernist writing. In the essay "The Literature of Exhaustion" (1967), Barth diagnoses an "exhaustion" of literature, which supposedly makes it mandatory for authors to use existing texts in order to produce original works. Only through positioning older texts in new contexts can genuine and fresh literature emerge. Influenced by the Argentinian writer Jorge Luis Borges (1899–1986), coupled with notions of the "death of the author" by the French theorist Roland Barthes, John Barth postulates a postmodern manifesto, which at the same time becomes an obituary for the traditional author function in literature.

Toward the close of the twentieth century, **Paul Auster** (1947–) continues postmodern American fiction in an attempt to simultaneously adhere to and resist a realist narrative style. His *New York Trilogy* (1987) weaves together modernist elements akin to John Dos Passos's *Zeitgeist* documentation with the antidetective genre à la Thomas Pynchon's *The Crying of Lot 49*. Auster also plays with elements of Edgar Allan Poe's detective genre, the poststructuralist theories of Jacques Derrida, and the psychoanalysis of Jacques Lacan, in order to mix them with self-referential tropes of postmodern American fiction. For example, the protagonist slips into the role of a detective and shares the role of the author Paul Auster, who then, before the backdrop of contemporary New York, crosses different levels of reality and tries to decipher enigmatic signs.

Also set in late twentieth-century New York are **Bret Easton Ellis**'s (1964–) "yuppie novels," which turn out to be dismal character studies of Wall Street culture. His most famous novel, *American Psycho* (1991), narrates in the first person the perverse passions of the mass murderer and investment banker Patrick Bateman. Until the end of the novel it is not clear whether Bateman's detailed descriptions of cold-blooded murder and dismemberment are real or a figment of his imagination. Ellis pairs these abject depictions with parodies of 1990s consumerism and marketing culture. Elements such as torture, rape, cannibalism, and necrophilia continue a strand in American fiction that leads from Edgar Allan Poe's inside perspective of a killer and **Truman Capote**'s (1924–1984) fictionalization of an actual murder *In Cold Blood* (1966) to the recent television series *Dexter* (2006–2013) with a mass murderer as its protagonist.

Some contemporary authors around the turn of the millennium continue to use postmodern techniques, including **David Foster Wallace** (1962–2008) in his last novel *Infinite Jest* (1997), depicting a parodic and dystopian future for the United States. Overlong sentences with cryptic vocabulary, several hundred footnotes with sub-footnotes, mysterious films used as secret weapons to infantilize viewers, and multiple strands of narration that converge in a mysterious tennis academy embroider criticism of the media with autobiographical vignettes of the former tennis pro David Foster Wallace. In numerous obituaries after Wallace's premature death in 2008, which was most probably caused by depression, he was regarded as one of the major voices in American literature in the twenty-first century. In 2012, for example, he was nominated for the Pulitzer Prize for his unfinished and posthumously published novel *The Pale King* (2011).

Wallace's contemporary and friend **Jonathan Franzen** (1959–) deliberately breaks with the narrative tradition that is reminiscent of Vladimir Nabokov or Thomas Pynchon. Written in a realistic style, Franzen's novel *The Corrections* (2001) received numerous prizes. This portrait of the second half of the twentieth century unites, in a family Christmas celebration, three major strands of narrative, each revolving around one child of the family. Already with his "Perchance to

Dream," published in 1996 in *Harper's Magazine*, Franzen had managed to raise his voice on literary theoretical issues, when taking a position against older manifestos by Philip Roth, Tom Wolfe, and Flannery O'Connor.

To take a stance against postmodernism, or to resist its mode of storytelling, is not a singular phenomenon and is by no means revolutionary. For example, the extremely successful novelist **John Updike** (1932–2009) had remained faithful to a realist style in all of his *Rabbit* novels (1960–2001) – a literary portrait of the 1960s, '70s, and '80s – despite the fact that he was writing his novels during the heyday of postmodernism.

9 Ethnic voices

Another tradition of American literature in the second half of the twentieth century runs mostly parallel to postmodernism but is relatively untouched by its often playful narrative techniques. Only in the last few decades has literary criticism started to pay attention to ethnic voices within the United States. Texts by African Americans, Latinas and Latinos, Asian Americans, and Native Americans have been grouped as separate literary traditions and fields of academic inquiry – a development of "ghettoizing" literature that is not unproblematic. For example, to simply categorize Ralph Ellison's novel *Invisible Man* (1953) as a milestone in the evolution of the African-American novel would not do justice to its position within the tradition of the American novel as such. Despite this problem, it nevertheless makes sense to trace some of these ethnic traditions individually.

While mid-twentieth-century African-American novels often gravitate around male stories of initiation, such as **Richard Wright**'s (1908–1960) *Native Son* (1940) and **James Baldwin**'s (1924–1987) *Go Tell It on the Mountain* (1953), later fiction tends to emphasize female protagonists and their concerns. **Alice Walker**'s (1944–) epistolary novel *The Color Purple* (1982) about an abused 14-year-old black girl in the South of the 1930s was groundbreaking. The novels of the Nobel Prize-winner **Toni Morrison** (1931–) contributed widely to the status of the African-American novel in general, while at the same time strengthening a female voice in fiction. Morrison's *Beloved* (1987) tells the drama of a black family in nineteenth-century slave culture. The novel keeps coming back to a moment of crisis in the family's past. On the run from slavery, Sethe had killed her daughter to prevent her from falling into the hands of their persecutors, thus "liberating" her from impending slavery. The family is consequently haunted by what seems to be a ghost-like reincarnation of the dead girl, a motif that is reminiscent of magical realism in Latin American literature.

The beginnings of African-American literature are intricately connected to biographical topics and the oral tradition of storytelling. Native American literature shares these features, which until today form an undercurrent in all genres of this tradition. With his Pulitzer Prize-winning novel, *House Made of Dawn* (1968), the Kiowa-Cherokee author **N. Scott Momaday** (1934–) managed to write himself into American literary history, projecting autobiographical and fictional elements onto his protagonist Abel. In a similar spirit, the Laguna-Pueblo author **Leslie Marmon Silko** (1948–), in her novel *Ceremony* (1977), focuses on a male Native American protagonist who was returning from World War II after traumatizing experiences. In his attempt to reintegrate into "normal" life, he faces typical Native American "problems," such as alcoholism and segregation by white society. Even more strongly than Momady, Silko works with the notion of a Native American oral tradition as a major motif in her novel.

Although Native Americans inhabited the New World prior to the European settlers, their legal position in many ways resembles that of African Americans. How long Native Americans were seen as an alien element within the United States becomes apparent in the long-standing legal discrimination against the indigenous population. Native Americans had to wait until 1924 to receive US citizenship. Until then, their status was that of a separate nation within the territories of the United States without sharing the rights of United States citizens.

Parallel to Native American writers Chicano and Chicana authors of Hispanic origin also became a very strong voice in the literary landscape of the second half of the twentieth century. In addition to the novelists **Ana Castillo** (1953–) and **Sandra Cisneros** (1954–), **Luis Valdez** (1940–) with his "Teatro Campesino" and plays like *Los Vendidos* (1967) highlighted the role of Mexican immigrants in the United States as early as the 1960s.

The second half of the twentieth century is also marked by a steady increase of literature by Asian-Americans, who, during World War II, the Korean War, and the Vietnam War, held a very problematic position within American society. **Maxine Hong Kingston**'s (1940–) feminist novel *The Woman Warrior* (1975), which deals with gender issues that go far beyond ethnic aspects, together with **Amy Tan**'s (1952–) *The Joy Luck Club* (1989) and its successful screen adaptation, helped Asian-American authors to become an integral part of mainstream American literature.

Traditional American literary history also considers the works of Jewish-American authors as a relatively independent tradition. One of its major representatives is **Saul Bellow** (1915–2005), with his existentialist novel *Dangling Man* (1944) about a young man who escapes his identity crisis by voluntarily enlisting in the army. Bellow's most successful novel, *Herzog* (1964), equally revolves around the mental crisis of a male protagonist, in this case the scholar Moses Herzog, who drafts letters to living and dead persons alike in order to get a grip on his life. Unlike other Jewish authors, Bellow does not necessarily foreground Jewish topics. A number of Jewish authors approach Jewish issues and concerns in a much more direct manner, like **Isaac Bashevis Singer** (1902–1991) in his short story "Gimpel the Fool" (1957), **Bernard Malamud** (1914–1986) in his story collection *The Magic Barrel* (1958), and **Cynthia Ozick** (1928–) in her experimental prose. **Philip Roth** (1933–), in his *Zuckerman* novels (1974–2007), stylizes Jewishness on a metafictional level via the figure of the Jewish writer Nathan Zuckerman. **Jonathan Safran Foer** (1977–) continues this tradition of metafiction paired with trauma in his post-9/11 novel and film adaptation *Extremely Loud and Incredibly Close* (2005).

How eagerly American popular culture absorbs Jewish writing is demonstrated by the success of the novels and film scripts of **Richard Price** (1949–). His realistic dialogues made him a much sought-after Hollywood author in the 1980s, with several Oscar nominations. Cooperation with the African-American filmmaker Spike Lee for the film *Clockers* (1995) and the film scripts for several seasons of the cult television series *The Wire* (2002–2008) make Price one of the most widely received American writers. New television series like *The Wire*, *Dexter* (2006–2013), and *Mad Men* (2007–), whose plotlines often span more than one season, increasingly adopt the traditional narrative

Ethnic voices 109

Figure 9.1 DVD cover of *The Wire* (season 1).

forms of epic cinema or the novel. Hollywood has always employed canonical authors, such as William Faulkner or Sam Shepard, for film scripts or adapted their texts for movies. More recently, however, major premium television channels have been commissioning famed writers, including the Jewish-American author Richard Price, for their epic-like series, which in turn provide an unprecedented, global platform for American literature in new media formats.

* * *

The texts of ethnic groups, which literary history increasingly focused on in the last decades of the twentieth century, especially highlight one of the leitmotifs of American literature in general. From its earliest manifestations in the colonial period to the present day, American literature seems to have concerned itself with the concept of the "Other." The alien, foreign, or new has served as a basis for literary production and self-definition, as well as an element of creative friction. It manifests itself in the role of the New World with its alien indigenous peoples in colonial or frontier literature. It also encompasses one's own "otherness," as in the Puritan spirit of being the chosen or select, and is the republican antipode to monarchism in the political transformations of the late eighteenth century. The sublation or obliteration of the Other, as advocated in the merging of subject and object in transcendentalism, is another variant of this phenomenon, as is the attempt to bring together the races in the literature of the Civil War period. Similarly, the friction between America and Europe in the novel of manners in realism, as well as naturalism's turn toward the underside of society, are, in the widest sense, expressions of American literature coming to terms with otherness. Even modernism's attempts to implement new media into literary discourse, such as painting and film, manifest American literature's interest in the Other on a structural level. Simultaneously, modernism opens up to the ethnic Other, as, for example, in stylizing African and African-American culture as a rejuvenating force in the genres of the novel and drama after World War I.

Literary history's privileging of ethnic voices in the latter part of the twentieth century, therefore, continues a latent deep structure within American literature, which has been creatively negotiating otherness from its very beginning. Although similar phenomena may also be at work, to a certain extent, in other national or colonial literatures, this high degree of tension between identity and alterity seems to be typical for American literature as such, and is largely responsible for its idiosyncratic character.

10 Literary theory in the United States

Literary production always goes hand in hand with a critical reception of texts or the emergence of theoretical discourses on literature. In the case of American literary history as a comparatively young tradition, the scholarly and methodological reflection on literature took some time to fully develop. Prior to the twentieth century it is difficult to isolate literary theory in the narrow sense of the term as a philosophy of science that deals with the methods and objectives of literary analysis. While England, together with the rest of Europe, produced treatises on the nature of literature – with authors such as Philip Sidney (1554–1586), John Dryden (1631–1700), and Matthew Arnold (1822–1888) – as early as the Renaissance, North America had lagged behind in this respect by its lack of larger self-contained theoretical texts.

However, this does not mean that American writing did not reflect on literature from a theoretically informed vantage point in earlier periods. On the contrary, American authors, as we have seen in previous chapters, very often used the prefaces to their works to implicitly concern themselves with major questions on the nature and role of literature with respect to North America. Such instances of **authorial self-reflection** include the proem to Anne Bradstreet's (*c.*1612–1672) poems, in which she situates herself as a female author in a patriarchal colonial tradition. In an analogous move Phillis Wheatley (1753–1784), in the opening lines of her collection of poems, problematizes her role as an African-American slave and poet under white supremacy. Charles Brockden Brown's (1771–1810) reflections on the genre of the Gothic novel for an American setting, in the preface to his novel

Edgar Huntly (1799), attempt to come to terms with the question of European influence in contrast to what is distinctly American in the emerging literature of the Early Republic. In a similar vein the transcendentalists in the nineteenth century continue to stress the uniqueness of American literature. Ralph Waldo Emerson (1803–1882), in his philosophical essays, for example, touches on literary production and reception when he advocates a fresh and unobstructed reading and writing of literature as an expression of American individualism as well as an act of emancipation from European models. Following Emerson's lead, Walt Whitman (1891–1892), in the preface to *Leaves of Grass* (1855), proclaims the nature of the American poet as the physical embodiment of American literature and culture.

But American authors do not just pursue questions connected with the construction of a national American literary identity and tradition. In his essays "The Philosophy of Composition" (1846) and "The Poetic Principle" (1850), Edgar Allan Poe (1809–1849) touches on more general aesthetic principles. For instance, he advocates a "unity of effect" in literature – a concept that will become a key issue with the school of New Criticism in the twentieth century. He also opposes didacticism in literature by propagating an early "art for art's sake" attitude. Poe even anticipates psychological approaches to literary texts when proposing the dead female body as an aesthetic fetish for literary production. Nathaniel Hawthorne (1804–1864), in his prefaces – for example, to *The Scarlet Letter* (1850) – also pursues more genre-related questions concerning the nature of fiction, attempting to contrast his notion of the romance with other forms of prose. For him, the romance possesses its own logic and is not necessarily tied to realism, which the traditional English novel adhered to when it emerged in the eighteenth century.

Toward the end of the nineteenth century the debate about what constitutes realism in fiction produced one of the first independent texts of literary theory. William Dean Howells's (1837–1920) *Criticism and Fiction* (1891), together with his columns in the *Atlantic Monthly* (1857–) and *Harper's Magazine* (1850–), codified the criteria for realism in the American novel for years to come. Fellow realist writer Henry James (1843–1916) solidified the notion of American realism in the prefaces to his novels as well as in independent theoretical treatises. In his famous essay "The Art of Fiction" (1884), many of his beliefs revolve around the necessity for realistic characters and subject matter in fiction while, nevertheless, demanding the largest possible freedom of choice for the author. Howells's and James's definitions of realism mark the beginning of treatises in the United States that are primarily geared toward providing clear-cut guidelines concerning what kinds of characters, plots, settings, and narrative techniques authors of "good" fiction should employ in their texts.

With the advent of modernism in the first decades of the twentieth century, this particular text type metamorphoses into programmatic manifesto-like writings that postulate rules or suggestions for the production of state-of-the-art poetry. Ezra Pound's (1885–1972) graphic guidelines for imagism as a condensed and highly structured form of lyric expression is a major example of the outburst of modernism's manifesto culture in literature and the arts in general. With Pound's fellow countryman T. S. Eliot (1888–1965) this highly prescriptive "how-to" mode gradually gives way to more analytical texts. Eliot's essays on general topics of literary history are in line with the overall formalist trends of the time and could be easily integrated into the omnipresent force of New Criticism that developed in the 1930s, as we will see later.

Before America engaged in the major theoretical approaches of international literary theory, **New Humanism** dominated the critical landscape in the first decades of the twentieth century with a debate concerning literature's relation to society. This distinctly American controversy revolved around the question of whether the main function of literature is educational or purely aesthetic, putting a strong emphasis on the moral use of literature for the development of a functioning society. These ideas are closely connected to the work of the literary critic Irving Babbitt (1865–1933), especially his book *Literature and the American College* (1908). The debate between New Humanists and antihumanists, who advocated a less morally grounded function of literature, went on for the first three decades of the twentieth century, directly or indirectly involving all of the major voices in American letters.

Most of the other forces of American literary theory in the twentieth and twenty-first centuries are either closely connected to European trends or exerted major influence on movements in Europe and the rest of the world. These various strands of modern literary theory generally fall into four main categories or overall approaches, focusing on the dimensions of author, text, reader, or context. Of course, every single interpretation and every theoretical approach to literature relies on the literary text as an object of inquiry. However, not every movement privileges the text in the same way. In some schools external, i.e. extrinsic factors, such as the author, reader, or the larger context of a work, move to the center of inquiry and play down the role of the text per se as a self-contained entity.

Author-oriented approaches

As early as the nineteenth century, **biographical criticism** evolved as an approach that privileged extratextual dimensions by establishing a direct link between the literary text and the biography of the author. Dates, facts, and events in an author's life are juxtaposed with literary elements of his or her works in order to find aspects that connect the biography of the author with the text. Research into the milieu and education of the author should ideally shed light on certain phenomena in the text. In addition, an author's library can provide insight into the author's background reading, or letters and diaries may reveal additional personal information.

In most cases, however, autobiographical material is encoded in the fictional text. The American playwright Eugene O'Neill (1888–1953), for example, used veiled autobiographical elements in his play *Long Day's Journey into Night* (c.1941; publ. 1956). Although the characters and events in the play are supposedly fictional, they are based on real people and dramatize events from O'Neill's family life. As we have seen in the cases of J. D. Salinger (1919–2010) and Thomas Pynchon (1937–), a number of authors and critics object to author-centered approaches to literature. Literary theory eventually took a clear position against biographical criticism. In his famous 1968 essay "The Death of the Author" the French theorist Roland Barthes (1915–1980) argued along these lines, claiming that the life and the intentions of an author are of no concern for the interpretation of a text.

While flourishing in the nineteenth century, the more traditional schools of biographical criticism lost momentum and changed direction under the influence of psychology after the turn of the century, partly sharing concerns with **psychoanalytic literary theory**. English translations of Sigmund Freud's (1856–1939) and C. G. Jung's (1875–1961) major works as well as visits to the United States by the two leading psychoanalysts influenced the way American critics approached literature and even the new medium of film in the first decades of the twentieth century. Under this influence literary criticism expanded the study of psychological features beyond the author to cover a variety of intrinsic textual aspects. In many instances fictional characters of a text became subjects of psychological analysis, almost as if they were real people. And psychoanalysis itself established a connection to literature. Sigmund Freud, for example, borrowed from literary texts in his explanations of certain psychological phenomena. Some of his studies, among them the analysis of E. T. A. Hoffmann's (1776–1822) short story "The Sandman" (1817), rank among the classic interpretations of literary texts. C. G. Jung, on the other hand, in his essay "On the Relation of Analytical Psychology to Poetry" (1922) explicitly adapted his own archetypal theory for the study of literature.

Among the first American publications that implemented a psychological framework for the study of literature was I. A. Richards's (1893–1979) *Principles of Literary Criticism* (1924). For Richards and his followers, literature acts as a reflection or representation of the mental realm and is therefore intricately interwoven with psychological processes. Over the next decades psychoanalytical criticism produced a number of studies that used Freud or Jung as their starting point. A landmark publication in this respect was Northrop Frye's (1912–1991) *Anatomy of Criticism* (1957), in which the Canadian critic applies C. G. Jung's notion of archetypes to the study of literature. Archetypal theory claims that larger mental concepts, which escape historical or cultural boundaries, govern human nature, similar to a collective unconscious, and thus lie at the heart of literary texts. Leo Marx's (1919–) *The Machine in the Garden* (1964), which discusses American culture suspended between the archetypal notion of paradise and technological progress, is part of this psychologically informed approach. In a similar move, although relying on Freudian concepts, Harold Bloom (1930–) in *The Anxiety of Influence* (1973) stylizes the Oedipal crisis as a governing mechanism in the struggle for success among authors, who continually strive to overcome the influence of father-like predecessors in literary history.

Between 1910 and 1920 early psychoanalytic theory also gave a boost to emerging film theory. The first major book on film studies, Hugo Münsterberg's (1863–1916) *The Photoplay* (1916), inaugurates psychological film theory by analyzing mental reactions and processes that take place when one watches a movie. Münsterberg and early film theorists regarded the spatial and temporal freedom of filmic storytelling to be very similar to the processes of the human imagination. A crucial observation for future film studies was their belief that inner, human reality can best be expressed through the medium of film.

Also linked to this psychological approach, but more strongly focused on the author, is **auteur theory**. Created and advocated by the American film critic Andrew Sarris (1928–2012) and the French filmmaker François Truffaut (1932–1984), this approach analyzes specific characteristics of great film directors. Like author-oriented approaches to literature, it views a director's *oeuvre* as an expression of his or her style. Targets of this methodology were major filmmakers, such as Orson Welles (1915–1985) and Alfred Hitchcock (1899–1980), whose individual styles invited this kind of analysis. However, the entire author-centered approach is problematic when it is applied to film. While literary authors are usually solely responsible for their works, a film director is only one of many people (screenwriter, actors, makeup artists, producer, etc.) who contribute to the creation of a movie.

Psychoanalysis has remained a crucial force in criticism and theory. In the later twentieth century, psychoanalytic criticism regained momentum under the influence of the French analyst Jacques Lacan (1901–1981), whose interpretation of Edgar Allan Poe's texts, for instance, had a major impact on Anglo-American literary theory. During the last decades of the twentieth century, Lacanian theory also heavily influenced feminist film theory. In the 1970s, Laura Mulvey's (1941–) essay "Visual Pleasure and Narrative Cinema" (1975) triggered an extensive discussion about the "male gaze" in film. According to Mulvey, traditional Hollywood cinema is based on the psychoanalytical processes of a male viewer, fragmenting and objectifying the female body into eroticized objects of the male gaze. This means that traditional Hollywood film – mostly through particular framings, camera angles, and editing features – singles out erotically charged female body parts for the visual pleasure of the male viewer.

The interest in psychological phenomena indirectly aided the spread of the so-called reader-centered approaches. Their focus on the reception of a text by a reader or on the reading process can, therefore, also be seen as an investigation of psychological phenomena in the widest sense of the term.

Reader-oriented approaches

Indirectly influenced by psychoanalysis but more directly a reaction to the dominant position of text-oriented New Criticism, which we will discuss later, **reader-response theory** developed in the 1960s. The terms reception theory, reader-response theory, or aesthetics of reception are used almost interchangeably to summarize those approaches that privilege the reader's point of view. Reader-centered methodologies focus on the recipients of a text and investigate why, where, and when a text is read, at times also examining certain reading practices of social, ethnic, or national groups. Many of these investigations also deal with and attempt to explain the physiological aspect of the actual reading process. They aim to reveal certain mechanisms that are at work in the transformation of the visual signs on paper into a coherent, meaningful text in the mind of the reader.

Reception aesthetics in general and its American variant in particular are closely connected to the German literary theorist Wolfgang Iser (1926–2007), who also taught for a number of years in the American university system. One of his key arguments, for example, is that every text has an implied reader. The author writes, according to this concept, an abstract and ideal reader into his or her text, thereby shifting the attention from the real reading individual to a disembodied dimension of reception, intricately interwoven with the text itself. Reception aesthetics assumes that a text creates certain expectations in the reader in every phase of reading. These expectations are then fulfilled or left unfulfilled. Wolfgang Iser's term of the blank or "spot of indeterminacy" refers to the options stimulated by the text and consequently completed by the reader. Filling in these blanks depends on subjective individual traits as well as on more general features, such as education, age, gender, nationality, and the historical period of the recipient. The reader's expectation plays a role in every sort of text but it is most obvious in literary genres like detective fiction, which depend heavily on the interaction between text and recipient. Edgar Allan Poe's

(1809–1849) "The Murders in the Rue Morgue" (1841), for example, consists of several blanks of this sort, which consistently misguide the reader's imagination and expectation.

In the United States, reception aesthetics is very closely linked to the literary critic Stanley Fish (1938–), whose book on the baroque poet John Milton (1608–1674), *Surprised by Sin* (1967), marks the beginning of an American reader-oriented theory. Fish reads Milton's epic poem *Paradise Lost* (1667) from a reader's perspective, thus ascribing to the recipient the role of an active agent in the construction of the text rather than that of a passive consumer. Fish demonstrates how Milton renders Satan as a likable character in order to let the reader experience empathy for the devil and thereby makes the reader actively participate in the fall of Adam and Eve.

These reader-centered approaches were particularly influential in the 1970s as reactions to the dogmas of text-oriented New Criticism, which had dominated the critical landscape for a number of decades.

Text-oriented approaches

In the first part of the twentieth century, partly influenced and inspired by the Eastern European schools of Russian formalism and the Prague school of structuralism, the Anglo-American movement of **New Criticism** revolutionized literary criticism. Focusing on the text per se it emerged as a relatively monolithic school that dominated college and university education in American literary studies from World War II to the end of the 1960s. New Criticism derived its name in opposition to older critical attitudes. It turned itself especially against the dominant romantic self-indulgence prevalent throughout the nineteenth century, which tended to rely on subjective or emotional empathy by the critic rather than objective criteria in the analysis of texts. Irving Babbitt (1865–1933) with his book *Rousseau and Romanticism* (1919) became a spokesperson for this antiromantic attitude in the modernist period. I. A. Richards's student William Empson (1906–1984), in his book *Seven Types of Ambiguity* (1930), was one of the first to codify ideas that helped New Criticism to establish itself as the most dominant critical school in the twentieth century. Literary critics such as William K. Wimsatt (1907–1975), Allen Tate (1899–1979), and J. C. Ransom (1888–1974) represented this school, which maintained its status as an orthodox method for more than three decades. New Criticism takes a stance against evaluative critique, source studies, investigations of sociohistorical background, and the history of motifs; it also objects to author-centered biographical or psychological approaches as well as the history of reception. Its main concern is to free literary criticism of extrinsic factors and thereby shift the center of attention to the literary text itself.

New Criticism objects to two major fallacies in traditional analyses of texts. The term "affective fallacy" stigmatizes interpretive procedures that take into account the emotional reaction of the reader as an analytical tool. In this respect, New Criticism does away with the use of subjective emotional responses caused by texts. In order to maintain an objective stance, the critic must focus solely on textual characteristics. The term "intentional fallacy" criticizes interpretive methods that attempt to recover the original intention or motivation of an author while writing a particular text. New Criticism, therefore, does not try to match certain aspects of a literary work with biographical data or psychological conditions of the author; instead, its aim is the analysis of a text – seen as a kind of message in a bottle without a sender, date, or address – based solely on the text's intrinsic dimensions.

In its analyses, New Criticism consequently focuses on phenomena like multiple meanings, paradox, irony, wordplay, puns, or rhetorical figures, which – as the smallest distinguishable elements of a literary work – form interdependent links with the overall context. A central term that is often used synonymously with New Criticism is "close reading." It denotes the meticulous analysis of these elementary features, which mirror larger structures of a text. New Criticism thus also objects to the common practice of paraphrase in literary studies since this technique does not do justice to such central elements of a work, as, for example, multiple meanings, paradox, or irony.

The elements mentioned above that comprise close reading supposedly reflect or unearth a text's "unity," another key term of New Criticism. Poetry, in particular, lends itself to this kind of interpretation since a number of genre-specific features, such as rhyme, meter, and rhetorical figures, call attention to the closed or unified character of this genre. This is why New Criticism focuses predominantly on poems, explaining the different metrical, rhetorical, stylistic, and thematic features as partial aspects of the poem's unity.

Among the formalist schools, New Criticism particularly distinguishes itself by the rigidity of its rules for textual analysis. Its applicable methodology and clear guidelines are mainly responsible for the dominant position it held until the late 1960s in English and American universities. It was gradually pushed into the background by reader-oriented approaches as well as by newer text-centered schools.

These more recent text-oriented trends are often subsumed under the term **poststructuralism**, not only because they come after the above-mentioned structuralist schools, but also because they adapt structuralist methodologies for purposes that go beyond those originally intended approaches. **Semiotics**, the study of signs, belongs to the text-oriented literary theory of the 1970s and 1980s, approaching a text as a system of signs. One basis for these complex theoretical constructs is the linguistic model of Ferdinand de Saussure (1857–1913). The Swiss linguist starts with the assumption that language functions through representation, in which a mental image is verbally manifested or represented. Before a human being can, for example, use the word "tree," he or she has to envision a mental concept of a tree. Building on this notion, Saussure distinguishes between two fundamental levels of the sign by referring to the prelinguistic concept (in this case the mental image of a tree) as the "signified" and its verbal manifestation (the sequence of the letters or sounds T-R-E-E) as the "signifier."

mental concept or
signified (French *signifié*)

sound image or
signifier (French *signifiant*)

T-R-E-E

The American philosopher Charles Sanders Peirce (1839–1914) developed a similar but more complex model of language, relying on the triadic structure of "object," "sign," and "interpretant."

Building on the theories of Saussure and Peirce, semiotics is not necessarily interested in analyzing an individual text as such but in finding overarching elements and structures. According to these older structuralist schools, language or texts function in a way that resembles a game of chess. A limited number of signs, like the figures on a chessboard, only make sense when they are in a closed system. On their own, the individual elements or chess pieces lack the complex meaning that they receive through the system – that is, the chessboard, the other pieces, and the rules of the game. Language and text are viewed as parts of a system whose meaning is created by the interaction of its different signs as well as the internally distinct features of its elements. This model of explanation is based on the principle of binary opposition. The term refers to the elementary distinctness of linguistic signs that cause difference in meaning. In the minimal pairs "h*u*t" / "h*a*t" or "*p*ull" / "*b*ull," for example, only one letter or sound (phoneme) is responsible for differentiating between the meanings of similar combinations of letters.

A new and unconventional aspect of semiotics is its attempt to extend the traditional notion of textuality to nonliterary or nonlinguistic sign systems. Semiotic methods of analysis that originated in literary criticism have been applied to anthropology, the study of popular culture, advertisements, geography, architecture, film, and art history. The majority of these approaches emphasize the systemic character of the object under analysis. Buildings, myths, or pictures are regarded as systems of signs in which elements interact in ways that are analogous to letters, words, and sentences. Among the most famous semioticians is the Italian Umberto Eco (1932–), who, before becoming an internationally renowned novelist with *The Name of the Rose* (1980), had a career as a leading theorist in semiotics.

A practical example of the analysis of nonlinguistic sign systems is Roland Barthes's (1915–1980) semiotics of fashion. The French literary critic regards clothes or garments as systems of signs whose elements can be "read" just like the literary signs of texts. Fashion, as a manifestation of social relations, provides a good example of these mechanisms in a nonlinguistic system. The signs as such remain the same over the years, but their meaning varies when the relationships between them change. Thus, wide pants, short skirts, or narrow ties convey messages that differ from those they conveyed a few years ago.

Semiotics fell on fertile ground in the United States not only in literary studies but also in film theory. A major influence, for example, was the French film theorist Christian Metz (1931–1993). In *Film Language* (1974), he attempted to explain film as a language-like semiotic system, which is restricted by a number of media-specific codes that create filmic narration. Since the 1980s, literary and film narratology have been closely interconnected, as David Bordwell's (1947–) *Narration in the Fiction Film* (1985) or the works of Seymour Chatman (1928–) illustrate. The major achievement of these two American film theorists was that they adapted and questioned literary concepts like point of view or the role of the narrator and introduced cognitive theory to film studies.

Like semiotics, **deconstruction** does away with the signified and uses the verbal sign or signifier as the starting point of its analyses. According to the French philosopher Jacques Derrida (1930–2004), the main representative of deconstruction – who also held long-term teaching appointments in the United States – there is no metaphysical or ontological basis for language and meaning. The world we experience can only be perceived via language and even reality itself is considered to be a linguistic construct. This means that nothing exists outside of the text and that even our perception of the world is of a textual nature. In the 1960s, the American philosopher Richard Rorty (1931–2007) coined the term linguistic turn for his notion that language is not merely a tool to convey meanings and ideas but also the most basic precondition for thinking.

Deconstruction starts with the assumption that a text can be analyzed (destructed) and reassembled in the course of analysis (reconstructed). In this sense the text is not the same after its reconstruction, since the analysis of signs and their reorganization in the interpretive process is like a continuation of the text itself. Traditional divisions into primary and secondary literature therefore dissolve when one regards interpretation as an integral part of the text.

However, deconstruction does not provide clear-cut guidelines for the analysis of texts and is not considered to be a monolithic method or school. Despite the complexity of its philosophical bases, deconstruction developed into one of the most influential theoretical trends in literary criticism during the 1970s and 1980s and has continued to provide basic notions and terminology for recent publications on literature.

An important example is Derrida's concept of *différance*. While Saussure saw a "signified" (mental concept) behind every "signifier" (verbal manifestation) in order to explain meaning, deconstruction deliberately does away with the signified by privileging the interaction between signifiers. Sometimes the concept of an encyclopedia is used to explain how meaning is derived in this system of interdependent signs. Every entry or signifier is embedded in a network of cross-references, each of which in turn contains a number of further references. For example, if you look up the term "tree" in a dictionary, the given definition might be "plant bigger than a bush." We could consequently look up the explanation for "bush" and probably find it described as a "plant bigger than a houseplant" – and so on. The meaning of a specific term, therefore, evolves in the continuous process of referring to other terms or signifiers. The neologism *différance* conflates the words "deferral" and "difference," thereby pointing out both the constant "deferral" to other signifiers and the "difference" that necessarily distinguishes the various signifiers in the system from each other. According to this model of explanation, meaning is generated through reference and difference on the level of the signifier only. This system of explaining the production of meaning in language does away completely with the notion of an elusive and immaterial signified, focusing instead on the material level of the signifier.

Although there seem to be few direct implications for literary studies in Derrida's theories, his ideas and texts exerted a tremendous impact on literary criticism and theory in the United States. In Europe, particularly in France, deconstruction was a school of philosophy, but in the United States a more literature-based branch of deconstruction was introduced and fostered by the Belgian literary theorist and Yale professor Paul de Man (1919–1983). The movement was soon taken up by the other **Yale Critics**, including Harold Bloom (1930–), Geoffrey Hartman (1929–), and J. Hillis Miller (1928–), all of whom shaped the theoretical landscape of the 1980s. Similar to the way post-structuralism preserves structuralism while at the same time criticizing it, deconstruction built upon New Criticism. Paul de Man, for example, rejected the notion of a single, correct interpretation of a text and instead attempted to recover ambiguities and polysemies.

Deconstruction in general and the American branch in particular came to a sudden halt when, about a decade after Paul de Man's death, his anti-Semitic and pro-Nazi journalism during World War II became public. The situation did not improve when the major deconstructionists, many of whom had been close friends with de Man, tried to come to terms with this sensitive issue. In many ways the Paul de Man case, or the debate that evolved from it, paralleled the earlier discussion about the American poet Ezra Pound and his support of Mussolini's fascist political ideas during World War II. Both cases posed the question of whether the work of an author or critic can be divorced from his or her political convictions, or if a work can be a masterpiece even if the biography of its creator makes him or her unacceptable in terms of political correctness. What became apparent in the Paul de Man case was that deconstruction, as a primarily text-oriented approach that tended to exclude extratextual or extrinsic factors, was unable to come to terms with the historical fact that its major theoretical figure turned out to be a Nazi collaborator.

Another major deathblow to deconstruction and poststructuralist theorizing in general came from a different academic discipline. In a hoax essay entitled "Transgressing the Boundaries: Toward a Transformative Hermeneutics of Quantum Gravity" (1996) on the interrelation of poststructuralist theory and quantum physics, the physicist Alan Sokal (1955–) made clear that it is possible to fool the reviewers of top journals with theoretical nonsense. Despite the fact that his article was solely made up of critical blabbering and jargon, deliberately devoid of any substantial message, it passed the reviewing process and was published in a top theory journal. In a subsequent essay in another journal Sokal laid open his scheme of exposing contemporary theoretical discourse as a self-serving, incomprehensible, and partly nonsensical enterprise in academia today.

Already prior to these two controversies, critical theory within and outside of the United States had shifted its emphasis from text-centered to more context-oriented approaches that analyze literature not only from a structural point of view but place texts in a wider context.

Context-oriented approaches

The term "context-oriented approaches" refers here to a heterogeneous group of schools and methodologies that do not regard literary texts as self-contained, independent works of art, but attempt to analyze them within a larger context. Depending on the movement, this context can be history, social and political background, genre, nationality, race, class, or gender.

An important school that places literary works in the context of larger sociopolitical mechanisms is **Marxist literary theory**. On the basis of the writings of Karl Marx (1818–1883) and literary theoreticians in his wake, including Georg Lukács (1885–1971) and Antonio Gramsci (1891–1937), texts become expressions of economic, sociological, and political factors. Conditions of production in certain literary periods, as well as their influence on the literary texts of the time, feature as key factors of interpretation. At American universities, Ian Watt (1917–1999), in his book *The Rise of the Novel* (1957), for example, argues that, compared to previous centuries, eighteenth-century England had a new material basis for the production, dissemination, and reception of texts. A large and wealthy enough reading public, cheap printing presses, and efficient distribution gave rise to a new mode of remunerating authors through a royalty system and consequently produced the genre of the modern novel in England. The Elizabethan Age, for example, lacked these material preconditions and was still based on a patronage system, in which wealthy sponsors commissioned literary works. In such a climate the novel would not have been able to evolve as it did in eighteenth-century England.

A major influence on English and American literary criticism was the Frankfurt School, with the German Marxist theoreticians Theodor Adorno (1903–1969) and Jürgen Habermas (1929–). One of the most eminent practitioners in the United States is Fredric Jameson (1934–), whose works, including *Postmodernism, or, The Cultural Logic of Late Capitalism* (1991), combine Marxism with poststructuralist theory. Independent of the fall of the Eastern Bloc, Marxist literary theory has lost much of its former impact over the last several decades. Since the mechanisms of class, to which Marxist theory pays major attention, often parallel the structural processes at work in race and gender, younger schools focusing on these issues have partly adapted the theoretical framework provided by Marxist criticism.

One of the more recent developments in the field of contextual approaches, which is partly indebted to a Marxist methodology, is **New Historicism**, which arose in the United States in the late 1980s. It also builds on poststructuralism and deconstruction with its focus on text and discourse, but adds a historical dimension to the discussion of literary texts. Such interpretations would, for instance, view certain works by Shakespeare together with historical documents on the discovery of America, and then treat discovery itself as a text. History, therefore, is not regarded as isolated from the literary text in the sense of a "historical background" but rather as a textual phenomenon in its own right. For example, one of the leading figures in New Historicism, Stephen Greenblatt (1943–), has analyzed a colonial text of early American literature by Thomas Harriot (*c*.1560–1621), comparing the relationship between Europeans and Indians in this text with the structures of dependence in Shakespeare's play *The Tempest* (*c*.1611). As a result, the mechanisms of power prove to be deeply rooted cultural structures, which dominated the historical as well as the literary discourses of the time. New Historicism takes an approach similar to that of the poststructuralist schools by including nonliterary phenomena in the definition of "text," thus treating historical phenomena as it would treat literary ones. A key term in New Historicist analyses is "discourse," which becomes an umbrella term for mechanisms at work in both realms, the historical and the literary.

Related to New Historicism, although an independent movement that gained momentum in the 1990s, is the field of **cultural studies**, which has emerged as one of the most influential areas within literary studies, if not the humanities as a whole. Although firmly rooted in literary studies, this approach deliberately analyzes the different aspects of human self-expression, including the visual arts, film, television, advertising, fashion, architecture, music, and material culture, as manifestations of a cultural whole. In contrast to semiotics, which is interested in isolating nonliterary phenomena from a structuralist approach, cultural studies adopts a comprehensive perspective that attempts to grasp culture's multifaceted nature at large.

Even though there has been an increased interest in cultural studies recently, cultural approaches and methodologies have existed in the humanities for a long time. The Swiss art historian Jacob Burckhardt (1818–1897) in *The Civilization of the Renaissance in Italy* (1860), for instance, argued already in the nineteenth century that cultural production is a holistic phenomenon, spreading over different areas of art and politics. In the twentieth century, the English theorist Raymond Williams (1921–1988) in his book *Culture and Society* (1958) supported this view. His plea for an understanding of cultural differences takes into consideration the whole of cultural production rather than isolated details. This evidently context-oriented approach considers literature as an important, but not the only, manifestation of larger cultural mechanisms. Applying such an overarching approach to phenomena in recent cultural studies is partly indebted to the concept of "thick description" that the American Clifford Geertz (1926–2006) developed for the study of cultures in anthropology.

The turn to ethnic, racial, or cultural minorities in critical theory largely followed developments in literary production. Starting in the 1970s, literary criticism not only devoted more space to discussions of minority texts but also developed methodologies in order to come to terms with these literary and cultural phenomena. African-American literary theory took the lead with Henry Louis Gates's (1959–) *The Signifying Monkey* (1988), which employs poststructuralist theory to demarcate a black aesthetic. Similar efforts followed in Asian-American or Chicano/Chicana studies, always placing literary works within a larger theoretical framework, based on specific minority contexts.

Recent scholarly interest has been very much directed toward national, regional, or ethnic "minorities" – the term "minority" referring to a marginalized group within a more dominant society. Most noticeably, all of these newer approaches focus on the concept of the "Other." A groundbreaking publication in this respect was *Orientalism* (1978), in which the literary scholar and Columbia University professor Edward Said (1935–2003) analyzed the way that Western culture sees the Orient as the stereotypical "Other," i.e. how the West defines itself in opposition to a mostly imaginary Orient.

In the past few decades cultural studies in general and **postcolonial theory** in particular have put a strong focus on societies that have evolved out of former colonies. The Indian theorist and Harvard professor Homi Bhabha (1949–) is an important scholar in this field, who incorporates ideas of poststructuralism and deconstruction in his theory of culture and cultural identity. In *The Location of Culture* (1994) Bhabha views culture as a phenomenon determined by discursive forces of mimicry and hybridization. This kind of approach, similar to recent theories of gender, regards cultural identity as a process of construction and performance rather than a biologically or ethnically determined given.

The most productive and, at the same time, most revolutionary movement of the younger theories of literary criticism in general and the contextual approaches in particular is **feminist theory** and the gradual emergence of gender theory. In this evolution process gender-oriented literary theory borrowed extensively from a variety of schools, including author-, reader-, and text-oriented approaches. Over the past few decades it has established itself in most academic disciplines and has become particularly strong in the various branches of modern literary criticism.

Feminist literary theory in the United States is closely connected to forces in feminism as a political movement, starting with Margaret Fuller's (1810–1850) *Woman in the Nineteenth Century* (1845) as well as Charlotte Perkins Gilman's (1860–1935) *Women and Economics* (1898). From a similar vantage point Betty Friedan's (1921–2006) book *The Feminine Mystique* (1963) addresses the role of women in American society in the 1950s, which is characterized by material wealth and silent oppression.

Feminist literary theory of the time starts with the assumption that "gender difference" is an aspect that has been neglected in traditional literary criticism and, therefore, argues that traditional domains of literary criticism must be reexamined from a female perspective. At the beginning of this movement in the late 1960s, thematic issues, such as the portrayal of women in literary texts by male authors, stood in the foreground. These early attempts of feminist literary criticism concentrated on stereotypes or distorted portrayals of women in a literary tradition dominated by men. One of the main issues of this basically reader-centered attitude was the identification of the woman reader with fictional female characters in literary texts. For this reason, the early phase of feminist literary theory goes by the name of "images of women criticism."

The next phase in feminist literary theory, using historical and author-centered approaches, can be described as "feminist literary history" and "canon revision." Its primary goal was to establish a new set of standard primary texts by female authors. Feminist literary critics in the mid-1970s drew attention to neglected female authors in the literary canon and propagated a new literary history by focusing on an independent female literary tradition. Elaine Showalter's (1941–) *A Literature of Their Own: British Women Novelists from Brontë to Lessing* (1977) is a landmark publication in this field by an American academic. This kind of feminist literary criticism with a focus on the revision of the canon – for which Showalter coined the term gynocriticism – remained the dominant movement up to the late 1970s, when it weakened and diversified under the influence of French feminists.

With the American reception of French feminists – such as Hélène Cixous (1937–), Luce Irigaray (1930–), and Julia Kristeva (1941–), who have strong backgrounds in psychoanalysis and philosophy – the focus of feminist literary criticism in the 1980s shifted to textual and stylistic reflections. This movement in feminism views language as decidedly male. The French feminists try to avoid this phallogocentrism – a neologism based on 'phallus' + 'logos' (word) – by empowering the female body with creative potential. Accordingly, a specifically feminine kind of writing should manifest itself in differences in plot, content, narrative structure, and textual logic. This theoretical assumption is commonly referred to by the French term *écriture féminine* ("female writing").

Gayatri Chakravorty Spivak (1942–), who translated one of Derrida's major texts into English, combined French feminism with Paul de Man's concepts of deconstruction. This movement developed into feminist deconstruction and eventually led to **gender theory**, which produced one of the most distinctive paradigm changes in the field by shifting the emphasis from the role of the woman to the concept of gender (male and female) in general. In recent gender theory the object of analysis is no longer the female alone, but rather the interaction between the genders. An increasing number of male critics are now working on gender issues, thus integrating masculinity into gender studies. In accordance with these latest developments, the role of male and female homosexuality in literature and literary criticism has received a great deal of attention. In the early 1990s, this led to the development of queer theory, which looks at society and culture not merely from a homosexual angle but includes all notions of sexual identity that deviate from the established "norm" of heterosexuality. In literature, proponents of queer theory might, for instance, point out homophilic undercurrents in works that until now were assumed to be "straight" writing.

The most recent trends in gender theory incorporate concepts of deconstruction, thus questioning the entire notion of a stable gender identity, a discussion that was initiated by the American literary theorist Judith Butler (1956–). In her book *Gender Trouble* (1990), Butler approaches gender identity in a manner reminiscent of deconstruction. Gender is "constructed" and "performed" through a number of interacting elements within a societal system. The key term is "gender construction," according to which "man" and "woman" adopt the role of signifiers whose meaning or identity is construed through an interdependent network of other signifiers.

The latest development shows a comprehensive view of the importance of both genders in literary production and reception, as well as the notion that gender is the result of a discursive practice rather than biological determinism. The evolution of feminist theory into gender theory, with its shifting areas of attention, also shows that the distinction between text-, author-, reader-, or context-oriented approaches at times gets blurred and cannot be more than a crude grid for conceptualizing major trends.

What characterizes literary theory in the United States is that it has been closely connected to and influenced by European phenomena from the very beginning. As early as the self-reflections carried out by authors in the colonial period and the Early Republic, theoretical voices from within the United States fashioned their own positions in reaction to British or European literary models. Even when self-contained theoretical texts started to emerge as an independent text type in the periods of realism and modernism, much of the theorizing was carried out by American expatriates or authors who returned to the United States after long stays in Europe. The major theoretical forces within America during the first half of the twentieth century, including psychoanalysis, Marxism, and New Criticism, are greatly indebted to European phenomena that fell on fertile ground in the United States, but in turn influenced the European situation. Similarly, in the second half of the century, German reception aesthetic as well as French deconstruction and poststructuralism fueled related movements across the Atlantic and produced highly innovative areas of research. Conversely, the originally American schools of New Historicism and recent gender studies had a tremendous impact on Europe and the rest of the world. Similar to the overall development of literary production on the North American continent, literary theory in the United States has also evolved in constant friction and mutual exchange with European phenomena in order to produce its own distinct voice.

Extended glossary and study aid

This glossary is an alphabetically arranged overview of the most important terms and concepts in American literary history and theory. It can be used either as a reference section that provides extended definitions or as a way of testing and revising your knowledge after reading Chapters 1–10.

affective fallacy
This important term of the school of New Criticism in the twentieth century objects to interpreting a text based on its subjective effect. It considers the reader's emotional reactions to be irrelevant to the scholarly analysis of a text.

African-American literature
Starting with the colonial period in the eighteenth century, African-American authors have contributed to American literary history, including the poetry of Phillis Wheatley (1753–1784), followed by the slave narratives of Olaudah Equiano (c.1745–1797), Frederick Douglass (1818–1895), and Harriet Jacobs (1813–1897). In the twentieth century, African-American self-expression in the social sciences, led by W. E. B. Du Bois (1868–1963) and Booker T. Washington (1856–1915), fueled the literary activity of the Harlem Renaissance in the 1920s, including the poet Langston Hughes (1902–1967) and the novelist Zora Neale Hurston (1891–1960). In the mid-twentieth-century, "black" writing developed into a distinct African-American tradition with Richard Wright (1908–1960), James Baldwin (1924–1987), and Toni Morrison (1931–) in fiction; Lorraine Hansberry (1930–1965) and Amiri Baraka (1934–) in drama; and Gwendolyn Brooks (1917–2000) and Nikki Giovanni (1943–) in poetry.

alienation effect
According to the German playwright and drama theoretician Bertolt Brecht (1898–1856), the alienation effect should guarantee that in dramatic performances, actors – and, above all, the audience – maintain a critical distance from the play. They are thereby reminded of the artificial and illusory nature of a theatrical performance. This can be achieved, for example, when an actor suddenly turns away from his interlocutors onstage and addresses the theater audience directly in order to comment on the action of the play.

American Renaissance
The literary scholar F. O. Matthiessen (1902–1950) coined this name for mid-nineteenth-century literature in the United States, roughly covering the decades from the 1830s to the 1860s. The writers whose work constituted this movement were concerned with writing a national narrative and interrogating national ideals and the failures of American democracy. Works and authors of the period largely overlap with transcendentalism but also comprise authors who were critical of transcendentalism, including, for example, Edgar Allan Poe (1809–1849).

archetypal criticism
Based on the depth psychology of C. G. Jung (1875–1961), this approach analyzes texts according to collective motifs that appear in myth and literature (e.g. mother figure, paradise, trickster, etc.). These concepts, which escape historical or cultural boundaries, govern human nature, similar to a collective unconsciousness. A major example of applied archetypal criticism is Northrop Frye's (1912–1991) *Anatomy of Criticism* (1957), which uses the archetypal notion of the four seasons to explain major literary genres. Leo Marx's (1919–) *The Machine in the Garden* (1964), which discusses American culture suspended between the archetypal notion of paradise and technological progress, is also part of this psychologically informed approach.

Asian-American literature
Despite the fact that Asian-American immigrants had been producing literary texts as early as the nineteenth century, literary criticism only started to view this body of work as an independent area of American literature in the last decades of the twentieth century. Important Asian-American authors include Maxine Hong Kingston (1940–) and Amy

Tan (1952–) as well as the writer and literary scholar Shirley Geok-lin Lim (1944–).

auteur theory

This movement in film theory, created and advocated by the American film critic Andrew Sarris (1928–2012) and the French filmmaker François Truffaut (1932–1984), views and analyzes a director's *oeuvre* – similar to author-oriented approaches in literature – as an expression of his or her particular style.

author-oriented approaches

This umbrella term refers to movements in literary criticism, as, for example, biographical criticism, that try to establish a direct connection between a literary text and the biography of the author.

autobiography

Despite ancient and medieval precursors, autobiographies in the modern sense of the term developed as late as the Renaissance. The genre of the American autobiography depends on two different strands of narratives, one being spiritual introspection, which is typical of Puritan writing with its strong affinity to self-analysis, as, for example, Jonathan Edward's (1703–1758) "Personal Narrative" (publ. 1765). This "spiritual" mode indirectly lives on in Benjamin Franklin's (1706–1790) *Autobiography* (1771–1790), Henry David Thoreau's (1817–1862) *Walden* (1854), and Henry Adams's (1838–1918) *The Education of Henry Adams* (1918). The other major force in American autobiography draws on texts about captivity or slavery, encompassing narratives of confinement by white Europeans, as, for example, Mary Rowlandson's (*c*.1637–1711) account of her abduction by Indians in the late seventeenth century, but also the major narratives by African-American slaves, including Olaudah Equiano (*c*.1745–1797), Frederick Douglass (1818–1895), and Harriet Jacobs (1813–1897).

Beat Generation

The term refers to a group of American writers in the 1950s and 1960s, including Jack Kerouac (1922–1969) with his drug-imbued "road novel" *On the Road* (1951), as well as Lawrence Ferlinghetti (1919–) and Allen Ginsberg (1926–1997) with their provocative poetry. The unconventional life and writing styles of the so-called beatniks, governed by sexuality and drugs, had a significant influence on the emancipatory counterculture of the 1960s in general.

Black Mountain School

This movement in poetry originated at Black Mountain College in North Carolina with Charles Olson (1910–1970), Denise Levertov (1923–1997), and Robert Creeley (1926–2005) as its main representatives. Charles Olson, in his essay "Projective Verse" (1950), called for an "open field" of composition in order to replace traditional closed poetic forms. Breath – and not rhyme and meter – should reflect the content of the poem and therefore be a poet's central concern. A poem's form needs to be based on the line, and each line should be a unit of breath and of utterance. Olson's essay, which deliberately places itself in the tradition of Ezra Pound's programmatic writing, assumed the status of a manifesto for the Black Mountain poets. In its short history this liberal arts college exerted a major influence on the American art and literature scene of the mid-twentieth century.

Chicano/Chicana literature

The term refers to texts written by Mexican Americans in the United States. Although early examples go back to the colonial period, the bulk of Chicano/Chicana literature evolved after the Mexican-American War in the middle of the nineteenth century when the United States annexed large territories in the Southwest that formerly belonged to Mexico. María Ruiz de Burton (1832–1895) is one of the first female representatives of Chicana writing published in English. In the second half of the twentieth century the novels of Ana Castillo (1953–) and Sandra Cisneros (1954–) as well as Luis Valdez (1940–) with his "Teatro Campesino" and his plays like *Los Vendidos* (1967), highlight the role of Mexican immigrants in the United States.

Chinese ideogram

The Chinese written character or ideogram was of major interest to the modernist American poet Ezra Pound (1885–1972), who regarded the pictorial nature of Chinese writing as an ideal medium for poetry. Pound's experiments with the haiku and his concept of imagism are directly connected to his preoccupation with Chinese pictographic writing.

close reading

This central term of the school of New Criticism in the middle of the twentieth century is often used as a synonym for intrinsic or text-immanent interpretation. It focuses on minute details of a text, trying to demonstrate how these elements create or support the larger unity of the text.

Colonial or Puritan Age

The period encompasses the seventeenth and eighteenth centuries in North America prior to the Declaration of Independence in 1776. Since most of the surviving literary texts of this era either have religious content or were produced by Puritans in New England, this period of American cultural and literary history is referred to as the Puritan Age. Major texts include William Bradford's (1590–1657) journal about the founding and early years of the Plymouth Colony, Anne Bradstreet's (*c.*1612–1672) collection of poems, reflecting on colonial everyday life from a female perspective, John Winthrop's (1588–1649) sermons on Puritan exceptionalism, Cotton Mather's (1663–1728) history of New England, Edward Taylor's (1645–1729) religious poetry, Jonathan Edwards's (1703–1758) flaming sermons, as well as the poems of the African-American writer Phillis Wheatley (1753–1784).

conceit

The term refers to a far-fetched metaphor that links two very different concepts. It was mostly used in England by the Metaphysical poets of the seventeenth century and also became a major feature of American Puritan poems and sermons. For example, in his poem "Huswifery" (publ. 1939), Edward Taylor (1645–1729) uses conceits when equating the tools of cloth production with a Christian believer. Similarly, Jonathan Edwards (1703–1758) employs conceits in his sermon "Sinners in the Hands of an Angry God" (1741) when comparing the sinner to a spider about to be thrown into a fire.

concrete poetry

This movement in poetry focuses especially on the visual form of a poem, including the shape and layout of letters, lines, and stanzas. Major examples in English literature are the pattern poems of the Metaphysical poets in the seventeenth century. By arranging the words on the page in a particular manner, they visually re-create objects, such as a church altar or the wings of a bird. In twentieth-century American modernist literature, the concrete poet e. e. cummings (1894–1962) even goes a step further by playing with the visual shapes of letters and punctuation marks.

context-oriented approaches
This umbrella term denotes various movements and schools in literary theory that approach a literary text not merely as an intrinsic, independent work of art, but as part of a wider context. The context can be historical (e.g. New Historicism), national (e.g. literary history), sociopolitical (e.g. Marxist literary theory), genre-specific (e.g. poetics), or gender-related (e.g. feminist literary theory).

cubism
This movement in painting during the first decades of the twentieth century focuses on innovative and unconventional visual perspectives. By abandoning the traditional central perspective in favor of a multiplicity of fragmented points of view, cubist painters, like Pablo Picasso (1881–1973), try to add movement to the static art of painting. For example, cubist paintings render an object with slight modifications several times on one canvas, each time only minimally changing the perspectival vantage point. Cubists thereby simultaneously fuse different moments in time or points in space into one composite image. Cubism received input through photographic and cinematic inventions, including editing and montage with their new possibilities of rapidly changing perspectives. Modernist writers, most prominently Gertrude Stein (1874–1946), then in turn used cubism as a model for literary innovation at the beginning of the twentieth century.

cultural studies
The movement originates with the English theorist Raymond Williams (1921–1988) and his book *Culture and Society* (1958), advocating a comprehensive view of different constituents of cultural production. The movement deliberately does away with notions of elitism concerning "high" or "trivial" culture. Cultural studies have gained momentum since the 1990s, viewing culture as a comprehensive discourse-based phenomenon, which shows striking structural analogies to trends in deconstruction and New Historicism.

Declaration of Independence
The Continental Congress ratified the document on July 4, 1776, announcing the independence of the thirteen colonies in North America from the British Crown. Drafted by Thomas Jefferson (1743–1826) and revised by Benjamin Franklin (1706–1790), the *Declaration*

clearly shows signs of Enlightenment philosophy with the concept of reason at the core of its argumentation. Its second sentence has become a major statement on human rights: "We hold these truths to be self-evident, that all men are created equal, that they are endowed by their Creator with certain unalienable Rights, that among these are Life, Liberty and the pursuit of Happiness." In 1863 this issue served as a key argument in the *Gettysburg Address* when President Abraham Lincoln (1809–1865) claimed that the American Civil War was unavoidable because the South had violated the doctrine of equality. One hundred years later, in 1963, Martin Luther King, Jr. (1929–1968), in his famous "I Have a Dream" speech, once again referred to the *Declaration of Independence* and Lincoln's *Gettysburg Address* – this time in order to propagate the African-American liberation movement of the 1960s.

deconstruction

This recent and complex poststructuralist approach is based on the works of the French philosopher Jacques Derrida (1930–2004). Like semiotics, it regards texts as systems of signs, but differs from traditional schools of structuralism by concentrating on the interaction of the signifiers (sound images), almost abandoning the concept of a signified (mental concept). The meaning of a word, according to Derrida, evolves in the continuous process of referring to other terms or signifiers. Deconstruction in the United States is closely connected to the Yale School with Paul de Man (1919–1983) as one of its major representatives.

différance

While traditional linguistics assumed a "signified" (mental concept) behind every "signifier" (verbal manifestation) in order to explain meaning, deconstruction deliberately does away with the signified by privileging the interaction between signifiers. "*Différance*," as a key term of deconstruction, is a neologism that conflates the words "difference" and "deferral," thereby pointing out this constant "deferral" to other signifiers and the "difference" that necessarily distinguishes the various signifiers in the system from each other.

discourse
This term refers to oral or written expression within a certain thematic framework, as, for example, historical, economic, political, or feminist discourse. In New Historicism, discourse becomes a concept subsuming literary as well as nonliterary texts of a period.

discovery and travel narratives
Accounts of discovery and travel mark the beginning of literature about America. Although these first documents differentiate little between geographic regions, mostly addressing the New World as a whole, they nevertheless anticipate tendencies of the later image of America in general and the image of the United States in particular. These early narratives paradoxically describe the new continent as a mixture of benevolent terrestrial paradise and dangerous wilderness. While early discovery accounts of the New World by Christopher Columbus (1451–1506) and Amerigo Vespucci (1452/54–1512) were largely influenced by ancient and medieval utopian literature, their travel narratives in turn influenced the revival of the genre of utopian literature, as, for example, Thomas More's (1478–1535) *Utopia* (1515).

Early Republic
The term refers to the period starting with the Declaration of Independence in 1776, when the North American colonies emancipated themselves from British colonial rule, to the consolidation of the United States of America in the first decades of the nineteenth century. The literature of the period is marked by an attempt to free itself from European and British models in order to find a voice of its own. Typical of the period are William Hill Brown's (1765–1793) and Hannah Foster's (1758–1840) sentimental novels, Charles Brockden Brown's (1771–1810) psychological fiction, Washington Irving's (1783–1859) short stories, and James Fenimore Cooper's (1789–1851) sea and frontier fiction.

Enlightenment
Influenced by the philosophy of John Locke (1632–1704) and Voltaire (1694–1778), this philosophical movement of the eighteenth century revolves around the concept of "reason." It attempts to free the individual from restrictions, manifests itself through religious tolerance, focuses on natural human rights, and propagates emancipation from oppression. With its orientation toward the future and its belief in

progress Enlightenment philosophy fell on fertile ground in America, functioning as an intellectual cornerstone of the American Revolution. Benjamin Franklin (1706–1790) and Thomas Jefferson (1743–1826) were influenced by the ideas of Enlightenment, which in turn manifested themselves in the self-fashioning of the Early Republic in documents such as the *Declaration of Independence* (1776) and the *United States Bill of Rights* (1789).

epic

This complex form of narrative poetry differs drastically from lyric poetry in length, narrative technique, portrayal of characters, and plot. At the center of an epic's complex plot traditionally stands a national hero who has to prove himself in numerous adventures and endure trials of cosmic dimensions. In the modern age, the epic has been overshadowed by the novel and lost momentum in the eighteenth century. Edgar Allan Poe (1809–1849), in his essay "The Philosophy of Composition" (1846), for example, discards the epic format as too long to produce what he calls a "unity of effect" (273). Despite being an unfashionable genre, American authors continued to produce epics, for example, Herman Melville (1819–1891) with *Clarel: A Poem and Pilgrimage in the Holy Land* (1876) or Ezra Pound (1885–1972) with his *Cantos* (1915–1962), which are modeled on the classical and medieval epics of Homer (*c*. seventh-century BC) and Dante Alighieri (*c*.1265–1321).

epistolary novel

This subgenre of the novel evolved in the eighteenth century parallel to the development of a functioning postal service. It relates the plot in first-person narration by using letters of correspondence as its medium. An early American example is Hannah Foster's (1758–1840) sentimental novel *The Coquette; or, The History of Eliza Wharton* (1797) about sexual seduction and the tragic death of a female protagonist.

ethnic voices

This umbrella term refers to literature written by ethnic minorities in the United States, including African Americans, Native Americans, Chicanos/Chicanas, and Asian Americans. Only in the second half of the twentieth century did mainstream literary criticism start to pay attention to these ethnic voices within the United States by developing specific theoretical methodologies for their analysis.

expressionism

Partly a reaction to realism, this movement in various fields of art and literature in the early twentieth century is characterized by exaggerated features of the "object" portrayed (e.g. strong lines in painting or the emphasis on types in the characterization of figures in literature). These elements are at work in Eugene O'Neill's (1888–1953) play *The Emperor Jones* (1920) with its expressionistic use of drums to magnify the heartbeat of the protagonist and thus to represent his increasing excitement. Elmer Rice (1892–1967) in *The Adding Machine* (1923) uses expressionist elements in stage design, such as specific lighting, and renders his characters with mask-like features as modes of representing the alienated identity of modern man. Expressionism in literature is closely connected to the German expressionist film of the 1920s.

feminism

A major early voice in American feminism is Margaret Fuller (1810–1850) with *Woman in the Nineteenth Century* (1845). She follows the tradition of French feminist Olympe de Gouges (1748–1793), who, toward the end of the eighteenth century, commented on the idea of equality in the French Revolution by testing its applicability for women. In her feminist critique, Fuller marks the beginning of a long tradition of American feminists who discuss women's roles in larger philosophical or economic contexts, including Charlotte Perkins Gilman (1860–1935) toward the end of the nineteenth century and more recently Betty Friedan (1921–2006) with her analysis of women in American society of the 1950s and 1960s.

feminist literary theory

This movement encompasses approaches in the second half of the twentieth century whose different methodologies focus on the female gender as a starting point for literary analysis. It evolves in phases, including "images of women criticism," which analyzes the representation of female characters in literary texts, "canon revision" in the 1970s, which adds female authors to traditional literary history, and French feminism with its emphasis on *écriture féminine* as a distinctly female mode of writing. Since the 1990s feminist literary theory has developed into gender theory, now focusing on aspects of gender constructions (male and female) and their impact on literature.

figural narrative situation

In texts that use this kind of narrative situation the narrator moves into the background, suggesting that the plot is revealed solely through the actions of the characters in the text – the readers "see" through the eyes of a character. This technique is a relatively recent phenomenon that developed with the rise of the modern novel, mostly as a means of encouraging the reader to judge the action without an intervening commentator. Henry James (1843–1916) in his novels often describes a person's state of consciousness from a so-called figural point of view.

film theory

As the theoretical and methodological foundation of film studies, film theory partly parallels developments in literary theory, but in general pursues its own media-specific goals. During World War I, psychological film theory, including Hugo Münsterberg's (1863–1916) *The Photoplay* (1916), analyzed mental reactions and processes that take place when we watch a movie, claiming that film can represent the workings of the human mind and the human imagination better than any other artistic medium. Around the same time, as part of Russian Formalism, Russian director Sergei Eisenstein (1898–1948) argued that montage – an editing technique that brings together seemingly unrelated and often discordant images – can create specific scenes in a viewer's mind. Building on montage theory, formalists in the 1930s also insisted that sound corrupts the artistic qualities of film. In contrast to the Russian formalists, the realism movement after World War II, including Siegfried Kracauer (1889–1966), regarded *mise-en-scène* and screen layout as the basis of an illusionary filmic reality. The auteur theory, which was created and advocated by the American film critic Andrew Sarris (1928–2012) and French director François Truffaut (1932–1984), analyzes specific characteristics of great filmmakers. Like author-oriented approaches, it views a director's *oeuvre* as an expression of his or her style. In the second half of the twentieth century, Christian Metz's (1931–1993) *Film Language* (1963) tried to explain film as a language-like, semiotic system, which is restricted by a number of media-specific codes that create filmic narration. In the 1970s Laura Mulvey (1941–) triggered an extensive discussion about the "male gaze" in film and initiated a gender-oriented film theory. Since the 1980s, film narratology, including the works of David Bordwell (1947–) and

Seymour Chatman (1928–), has focused on the question of a filmic narrator and narration in film.

first-person narration
We speak of a first-person narrative if one of the characters who is part of the story tells the story, referring to himself or herself in the first person singular. A famous example of a first-person narration by the protagonist in American literature is Mark Twain's *The Adventures of Huckleberry Finn* (1884), which lets the reader see the world through the eyes of an uneducated social outcast. Herman Melville's (1819–1891) *Moby Dick* (1851) uses a first-person narration by a minor character, the sailor Ishmael, in order to add to the mysteriousness of the protagonist Captain Ahab.

formalism
Often used synonymously with structuralism, formalism characterizes text-oriented approaches in the first half of the twentieth century, which focus on the structural aspects of a literary work, such as phonetic structures, rhythm, rhyme, meter, and sound. The most important schools are Russian formalism and the Prague school of structuralism.

Frankfurt School
This Marxist school, represented by the German theoreticians Theodor Adorno (1903–1969) and Jürgen Habermas (1929–), exerted a major influence on English and American Marxist literary criticism in the second half of the twentieth century.

French feminism
This feminist movement, which developed in France and became popular in the United States in the 1980s, stresses that traditional language and literature are decidedly male. It therefore advocates the use of a specifically feminine kind of writing (*écriture féminine*) that manifests itself in plot, content, narrative structure, and textual logic.

gender theory
Unlike older feminist literary theory, this relatively recent movement of the 1990s, based on the works of Judith Butler (1956–), no longer focuses exclusively on women, but includes issues concerning both genders in the interpretation of literary texts. Gender is no longer seen as a biologically given, but rather as a socially constructed concept that heavily relies on performativity.

Gilded Age

Mark Twain (1835–1910) mockingly referred to the literary period from the 1870s to the turn of the century, which largely coincided with realism, as the "Gilded Age." It implies an allegedly Golden Age, which, upon closer inspection, turns out to be only gilded on the surface and is, in fact, hollowed out by growing capitalism and materialism. It is the time of monopolized capital in new industries, such as the extraction of raw materials, the railroad, or telecommunications.

Gothic novel

This subgenre of the novel with an eerie, supernatural setting was particularly popular in late eighteenth-century England. Charles Brockden Brown (1771–1810) tried to adapt the genre for the American situation with his novel *Edgar Huntly, Or, Memoirs of a Sleepwalker* (1799).

Great Awakening

In the middle of the eighteenth century, the Puritan clergy in New England prolifically propagated a radical religious renewal called the "Great Awakening." One of its charismatic preachers was Jonathan Edwards (1703–1758), who gathered several hundred believers in a short amount of time, sending them into religious raptures with sermons such as "Sinners in the Hands of an Angry God" (1741). The movement combines traditional Calvinist concepts of predestination with ideas of Enlightenment philosophy.

haiku

This Japanese short poem consists of seventeen syllables divided into three lines (5, 7, 5) and tries to capture one specific image through a highly focused and condensed mode of expression. In the early modernist period, the American poet Ezra Pound (1885–1972) was fascinated by the condensed haiku format and used it for his idea of imagist poetry. In his most famous poem, "In a Station of the Metro" (1913), Pound reduces the crowd in a subway station to a single image of a wet branch with blossoms, thereby also evoking seasonal references as another typical feature of the haiku.

Harlem Renaissance

The term refers to an upsurge of African-American self-expression in America in the 1920s. In literature it continued the tradition of

African-American intellectuals around the turn of the century, such as W. E. B. Du Bois (1868–1963) and Booker T. Washington (1856–1915). Drawing on this climate of African-American self-expression in the social sciences, authors such as Langston Hughes (1902–1967) became important poets of the Harlem Renaissance in the 1920s, many of whom contributed to Alain Locke's (1885–1954) landmark verse anthology *The New Negro* (1925). Female African-American authors, such as Zora Neale Hurston (1891–1960) or Nella Larsen (1891–1964), captivated audiences with self-confident women protagonists. At the same time, the African-American writer and film director Oscar Micheaux (1884–1951) made numerous films with an all-black cast for a specifically black audience. During the Great Depression and the race riots at the beginning of the 1930s, the Harlem Renaissance lost momentum, finding a continuation in somewhat different, more fragmented but equally influential African-American voices in the second half of the twentieth century.

homiletic prose

A large amount of Puritan writing is characterized by sermon-like prose that dominates the literary output of colonial America in its early phase. Major examples of homiletic prose include John Winthrop's (1588–1649) *A Model for Christian Charity* (1960), which propagates America as the chosen colony, and Jonathan Edwards's (1703–1758) apocalyptic sermon "Sinners in the Hands of an Angry God" (1741).

imagism

Modeled on the Asian poetic genre of the haiku, which compresses and condenses an object to an image, Ezra Pound (1885–1972) founded a lyrical movement called imagism. Its cornerstone is Pound's definition of an image as an "emotional complex in an instant of time" (4). Imagism had a major influence on other modernist poets, including Hilda Doolittle (1886–1961) and T. S. Eliot (1888–1965).

implied reader

According to the German reception theorist Wolfgang Iser (1962–2007), the author writes an abstract or ideal reader into his or her text. The concept of the implied reader shifts the attention from the real reading individual to a disembodied dimension of reception, intricately interwoven with the text itself.

intentional fallacy
This important term of the school of New Criticism in the twentieth century objects to judging a text on the basis of the author's intention. It discards interpretations that try to reconstruct the author's original goals when writing a text; instead, it favors intrinsic aspects of the text.

Jamestown
The colony of Jamestown, founded in 1607 on the James River in Virginia, became the first successful permanent English settlement in North America. The first phase of the Jamestown experiment was closely connected to Captain John Smith (*c.*1580–1631), whose negotiating skills and ability to barter for food with the native tribes guaranteed the survival of the colony. During the first months of settling activities, Captain John Smith led exploratory trips, hoping to find gold in the surrounding areas of the Chesapeake Bay. At times these activities led to armed conflict with the native tribes.

Jazz Age
The decade after World War I, before the Great Depression in 1929, is also referred to as the Golden Twenties or the Roaring Twenties. The period is characterized by prohibition and an ensuing rise in illegal liquor business, a new self-confidence of women, new fashion styles, as well as the popularization of jazz as a form of entertainment. F. Scott Fitzgerald's (1896–1940) novel *The Great Gatsby* (1925) is a *Zeitgeist* picture of the Jazz Age with its exuberant parties and excesses.

Jewish-American literature
While Jewish authors have always contributed to traditional American literary history – especially in the twentieth century – Jewish-American literature has established itself as a relatively independent object of inquiry over the past few decades. Most important are Jewish-American novelists, including J. D. Salinger (1919–2010), Saul Bellow (1915–2005), Norman Mailer (1923–2007), Bernard Malamud (1914–1986), Isaac Bashevis Singer (1902–1991), Philip Roth (1933–), Paul Auster (1947–), and Jonathan Safran Foer (1977–). Many protagonists of Jewish-American novels are characterized by the tension between their own Jewish heritage and the conflicting norms of American society.

literary theory
Also referred to as critical theory, literary theory functions as the philosophy of science in literature that reflects on the methods and objectives of textual analysis. Depending on their main focus of attention, the respective theoretical schools can be roughly grouped into text-, author-, reader-, and context-oriented approaches.

manifest destiny
This key element of American self-understanding is indirectly based on the Calvinistic principle of predestination. The concept culminates in the belief of the early colonists and settlers during the westward expansion of the nineteenth century that their progress in America and their subjugation of Native Americans were God's will. Even today, this notion of a nation chosen by God dominates the self-image of the United States and is still used to legitimize various steps in domestic and foreign policy.

Marxist literary theory
This school, based on the writings of Karl Marx (1818–1883) and other Marxist theorists, analyzes literary texts as expressions of economic, social, and political backgrounds. Material conditions of production in particular periods are examined with respect to their influence on literary writings of the time.

Mayflower Compact
On board the ship *Mayflower*, bound for Virginia but landing north of their planned destination, William Bradford (1590–1657) drafted the "Mayflower Compact." Settling in territories outside the jurisdiction of the Virginia Company, the Pilgrims assumed a certain "liberty" for themselves, claiming that no one could exercise control over them. This kind of miniature constitution, which the Puritans called a "civil body politic" (Bradford 76), appears as the seed of self-organization and thus as the starting point of the American democratic self-image.

McCarthy era
Spearheaded by the conservative senator Joseph McCarthy (1908–1957), United States politics in the first half of the 1950s engaged in anticommunist propaganda and persecution. In this period the United States accused left-wing intellectuals, artists, and filmmakers of being supporters of communism. This mass hysteria found its literary representation in Arthur Miller's (1915–2005) play *The Crucible* (1953).

metafiction

The American postmodern writer William H. Gass (1924–) coined the term in a 1970s essay entitled "Philosophy and the Form of Fiction." It denotes fiction about fiction, meaning self-reflexive literary texts that focus on their own literary elements, such as language, narrative, or plot structure. Although present in earlier novels, such as Miguel de Cervantes's (1547–1616) *Don Quixote* (1605, 1615), it constitutes a main feature of postmodernism.

Metaphysical poets

The term goes back to the English eighteenth-century poet and critic Samuel Johnson (1709–1784), who labeled a group of English poets of the seventeenth century the Metaphysical poets. The subject matter of poets such as John Donne (1572–1631), George Herbert (1593–1633), and Andrew Marvell (1621–1678) oscillates between the religious and the erotic but converges in their fondness of conceits, i.e. far-fetched metaphors or similes. Since some of the poets rely on Neoplatonist ideas, including the metaphysical nature of beauty and perfection, Johnson referred to them as the Metaphysical poets.

mind-tricking narratives

In contemporary film, "mind-tricking narratives," such as M. Night Shyamalan's *The Sixth Sense* (1999), are characterized by twist endings that make the viewer realize that up to this point he or she has been severely misinterpreting crucial aspects of the plot. Indirect literary precursors to this type of filmic narrative in literature are Edgar Allan Poe's (1809–1849) "tales of ratiocination" or Ambrose Bierce's (1842–1913) short story "An Occurrence at Owl Creek Bridge" (1890).

modernism

Modernism denotes a movement in the first half of the twentieth century, roughly covering the decades from World War I to World War II. Scholarship often refers to this period as the "era of time and space" because it intensely occupies itself with these two parameters of human experience. In the late nineteenth and early twentieth centuries, groundbreaking inventions in material culture reshaped people's way of thinking with respect to these two dimensions. The literary practice of the modernist era reflected, experimented with, and revolutionized the use of spatial and temporal aspects of narratives. This goes hand in hand with a strong general interest in psychological processes at the time, including Sigmund Freud's (1856–1939) interpretation of dreams or C. G. Jung's (1875–1961) exploration of archetypes. This new attitude in literature consciously borrows techniques from the visual arts, as, for example, Gertrude Stein's (1874–1946) cubist literary style or the expressionist features of Eugene O'Neill's (1888–1953) and Elmer Rice's (1892–1967) plays. Modernist fiction often uses unconventional and multiple narrative perspectives, as, for example, in the novels of William Faulkner (1897–1962), or employs stream-of-consciousness techniques, as does John Dos Passos (1896–1970) in his collage-like fiction. In poetry, major innovations are Ezra Pound's (1885–1972) concept of imagism and T. S. Eliot's (1888–1965) experiments with intertextuality.

narrative perspective
The term refers to the way a story is told. According to traditional narratology, a story can be presented through different narrative situations, including authorial, figural, or first-person perspectives.

narratology
Narratoloy is the study of narrative. Basically, there are two different types – story narratology and discourse narratology. Story narratology deals with the content (story) of a literary work (what is told – motifs, themes, symbols, etc.) while discourse narratology concerns itself with the plot (discourse) of a literary work (how it is told – narrative situation, order, duration).

Native-American literature
A great deal of the literary production of Native Americans prior to the twentieth century was passed on in oral form – a feature that is still intricately interwoven with Native American literary self-understanding today. In the second half of the twentieth century, American "Indian" voices contributed to the different genres of American literature. One of the earliest specimens of Native American drama is Lynn Riggs's (1899–1954) *Green Grow the Lilacs* (1931), whose musical adaptation *Oklahoma!* (1943) became a major Broadway success. With his Pulitzer Prize-winning novel *House Made of Dawn* (1968), N. Scott Momaday (1934–) managed to write himself into American literary history, projecting autobiographical and fictional elements onto his protagonist.

In a similar spirit, Leslie Marmon Silko (1948–), in her novel *Ceremony* (1977), focuses on a male Native American protagonist, who faces typical Native American "problems," such as alcoholism and segregation by white society.

naturalism

While American realism, with its major proponent Henry James (1843–1916), focuses on the inner world of the characters, naturalism tends to turn toward outer circumstances. This movement, partially influenced by journalism, focuses on the milieu as an object of realistic depiction as well as on the deterministic function of specific conditions of society, including social Darwinism, sexuality, capitalism, and consumption. Stephen Crane's (1871–1900) *Maggie: A Girl of the Streets* (1893) with its emphatic descriptions of desolate family backgrounds, alcohol abuse, and domestic violence becomes the paradigm for this new approach. Also concerned with socioeconomic issues are the novels of Frank Norris (1870–1902), which explore larger dimensions of capitalist America, as well as Theodore Dreiser's (1871–1945) focus on the new urban consumer society of the turn of the century.

New Criticism

Partly influenced by East European formalism of the first half of the twentieth century, New Criticism develops into the most important Anglo-American text-oriented school after World War II. New Criticism differentiates interpretation from source studies, sociohistorical background studies, history of motifs, as well as author-oriented biographical or psychoanalytic literary criticism and reception history. It wants to free literary criticism from extrinsic elements – that is, those outside of the text – and bring the focus back to the literary text as such. Key terms are affective fallacy, intentional fallacy, unity, and close reading.

New Historicism

This relatively recent approach, starting in the 1980s, builds on poststructuralism and deconstruction but also includes historical dimensions in the discussion of literary texts. It presupposes a structural similarity between literary and other discourses within a given historical period. The movement is closely associated with the American Shakespeare and Renaissance scholar Stephen Greenblatt (1943–).

New Humanism
This movement dominated the critical landscape in the United States in the first decades of the twentieth century with a debate concerning literature's relation to society. This distinctly American controversy revolved around the question of whether the main function of literature is educational or purely aesthetic, putting a strong emphasis on the moral use of literature for the development of a functioning society. The ideas are closely connected to the work of the literary critic Irving Babbitt (1865–1933) and his book *Literature and the American College* (1908).

noble savage
Early discovery narratives tend to ascribe features of primordial innocence to native inhabitants of the New World. Michel de Montaigne's (1533–1592) essay "On Cannibals" (1580) is one of the earliest theoretical manifestations of this notion that has become a leitmotif in American cultural history. Starting with the Pocahontas myth in the early seventeenth century, the trope of the noble Indian continues in later American frontier narratives and the Western as a filmic genre.

objective correlative
T. S. Eliot (1888–1965), in his essay "Hamlet and His Problems" (1919), introduces the term "objective correlative" and defines it as a "set of objects, a situation, a chain of events" that is able to create a "particular emotion" (145). The objective correlative bears a close resemblance to the conceit of the Metaphysical poets and exhibits parallels to Pound's concept of the image.

omniscient or authorial narrative situation
This narrative situation renders the action from an omniscient, i.e. all-knowing, God-like perspective by referring to the protagonist in the third person. The narrator is not a character in the story. Most classical epics use an authorial narrative situation.

picaresque novel
This subgenre of the novel recounts the episodic adventures of a vagrant rogue (Spanish: *pícaro*) or somebody who gets into trouble by breaking social norms. A major example in world literature is Miguel de Cervantes's (1547–1616) *Don Quixote* (1605, 1615). Following British examples, the American author Tabitha Tenney (1762–1837) wrote

her *Female Quixotism* (1801), an adventurous and satirical novel about a heroine who loses her grip on reality due to excessive reading.

Pilgrim Fathers

In 1607 the so-called Separatists – Puritan groups who did not concur with the Church of England – left England and temporarily stayed in the Dutch city of Leyden. During their sojourn in the Netherlands, the Puritans got permission to settle in Virginia through a patent of the London Virginia Company. Under the leadership of William Bradford (1590–1657), about a hundred "Pilgrims" reached Plymouth in the area of today's Massachusetts in the year 1620, where they founded the second major British colony on North American soil besides Jamestown, Virginia. These pioneers are frequently referred to as the "Pilgrim Fathers."

Pocahontas myth

During the first months of settling activities in Jamestown, Captain John Smith (*c*.1580–1631) led exploratory trips into the surrounding areas of the Chesapeake Bay, which at times created friction with the native tribes. One of these conflicts, which supposedly left John Smith in the hands of the Indians, went down in American history as the Pocahontas myth. Pocahontas (*c*.1595–1617), the daughter of the major Indian chief Powhatan (*c*.1547–*c*.1618), is said to have rescued John Smith from his impending execution by putting her own life on the line.

postcolonial literature

This term refers to texts from former colonial territories in the Caribbean, Africa, India, and Australia that have attracted the attention of contemporary literary critics. In the English context these texts are sometimes also referred to as "new literatures in English," Commonwealth literature, or Anglophone literatures.

postcolonial theory

In past decades literary theory has put a strong focus on societies that have evolved out of former colonies. The Indian theorist and Harvard professor Homi Bhabha (1949–) is an important scholar in this field, incorporating ideas of poststructuralism and deconstruction into his theory of culture and cultural identity. In *The Location of Culture* (1994) Bhabha views culture as a phenomenon determined by discursive forces of mimicry and hybridization. This kind of approach regards cultural identity, similarly to recent theories of gender, as a process of construction and performance rather than a biologically or ethnically determined given.

postmodernism

The term was coined by the French theorist François Lyotard (1924–1998) in *The Postmodern Condition: A Report on Knowledge* (1984), in which he proposes that the postmodern era (approximately post-World War II) is defined by the downfall of all metanarratives (e.g. Kantianism, Hegelianism, and Marxism, which all argue that history is progressive, knowledge can liberate us, and knowledge has a unity). Postmodernism is skeptical about absolutes, totalizing explanations, objectivism, and belief in truths. Relativism and subjectivism are key terms. In literature these notions are frequently expressed in an academic, often self-reflexive, or metafictional way. Some of the major proponents include the novelists Vladimir Nabokov (1899–1977), Thomas Pynchon (1937–), John Barth (1930–), and Paul Auster (1947–); the playwrights Edward Albee (1928–) and Amiri Baraka (1934–) as American representatives of the theater of the absurd; and the poet John Ashbery (1927–).

poststructuralism

Poststructuralism criticizes as well as continues the structuralist movement and reached its height in the late 1960s. What it particularly criticized was structuralism's ahistoricity and, therefore, it included historical contexts. Furthermore, while structuralism pointed out the binary nature of our world (man/woman, white/black, straight/gay, normal/insane), poststructuralism stressed the fact that one component of these binary pairs is always suppressed by the other (woman, black, gay, insane). Sigmund Freud's Oedipus complex and Jacques Lacan's mirror stage are key concepts in poststructuralist theories. Poststructuralism does not believe in an autonomous subject but believes instead that the notion of a controlling self is a mere illusion.

predestination

One of the most central tenets of American Puritanism is the principle of divine providence, developed from the writings of the Geneva reformer John Calvin (1509–1564). According to this belief, God has predestined, before a person's birth, whether the person will be saved or damned. Thus, the deeds of a person have no direct influence on his or her redemption since God has already predestined their fate. By differentiating between chosen and not-chosen people, this doctrine creates a highly exclusive sociopolitical dynamic.

primary and secondary literature

The term primary literature refers to a literary text – usually belonging to one of the three traditional genres of fiction, poetry, and drama; whereas secondary literature denotes writing *about* primary sources, including scholarly articles, essays, or book-length studies. In modernism and postmodernism, authors deliberately play with the boundaries between the two. For example, the modernist poet T. S. Eliot (1888–1965) in his poem *The Waste Land* (1922) uses footnotes and references to scholarly texts and the postmodernist writer Vladimir Nabokov (1899–1977) in *Pale Fire* (1962) applies the structure of a text edition of a poem to his novel.

Protestant work ethic

For Protestants – Calvinists in particular – to be chosen by God manifests itself in material success. Therefore, an inherent pursuit of financial wealth drives predominantly Protestant countries such as the United States. According to the German sociologist Max Weber (1864–1920), in his groundbreaking essay "The Protestant Ethic and the Spirit of Capitalism" (1904), this orientation toward individual success, legitimized by the concept of predestination, creates a capitalist tendency in countries with a high Protestant population.

psychoanalytic literary theory

Starting in the early twentieth century this movement applied the concepts of Sigmund Freud's (1856–1939) psychoanalysis and C. G. Jung's (1875–1961) depth psychology of archetypes to the analysis of literature. This approach gained momentum in the second half of the twentieth century under the influence of the French psychoanalyst Jacques Lacan (1901–1981).

psychological film theory

This branch of film theory uses psychological approaches for the analysis of film. While early psychological film theory focused on mental effects and processes when watching a film, later schools applied a psychological framework to the interpretation of the different elements of film.

Puritan interregnum
The term refers to a period of English history between 1649 and 1660 when the Puritan Oliver Cromwell (1599–1658) deposed the king and abolished the British monarchy. The Puritan Commonwealth is followed by the Restoration period, in which England became a monarchy again.

reader-oriented approaches
This umbrella term refers to schools whose methodology revolves around the reception of texts by readers. Reception history, for example, concerns itself with the diachronic, i.e. historical, aspects of how texts are received by the public, including reviews or sales figures of literary works. In contrast to this empirically informed method, reader-response theory concerns itself with the act of reading or the role of the reader from a theoretical vantage point.

reader-response theory
Also referred to as "reception theory" or "aesthetics of reception," this school of the second half of the twentieth century concentrates on the relation between text and reader. It stands in contrast to intrinsic or purely text-oriented approaches. The movement is indebted to the theoretical writings of the German literary theorist Wolfgang Iser (1926–2007).

realism
The last decades of the nineteenth century were characterized by an increasing preoccupation with a faithful depiction of reality in literature. Influenced by European writers, this concern culminates in the American writer and literary theorist William Dean Howells (1891–1920), whose manifesto-like program *Criticism and Fiction* (1891) demands that the novel reorient itself, using the quotidian and ordinary as its models. Howells's list of prerequisites for the realist novel encompasses untypified characters, simple language, nonmelodramatic plots without a standard happy ending, as well as a reduced authorial voice, emphasizing "showing" over "telling." Major works of the period include Mark Twain's (1835–1910) depictions of a social outcast in *The Adventures of Huckleberry Finn* (1884), as well as Henry James's (1843–1916) and Edith Wharton's (1862–1937) novels of manners set in upper-class society.

Roanoke or the Lost Colony

Roanoke is the earliest British colonial venture in North America on the Virginia coast (actually located in present-day North Carolina). In 1584 Queen Elizabeth I (1533–1603) granted Sir Walter Raleigh (c.1554–1618) a charter to found a colony in North America. It went down in history as the Lost Colony. Bad leadership, coupled with undiplomatic and even hostile contact with the Natives, made a permanent settlement difficult. The majority of the settlers had to be rescued by Sir Francis Drake (c.1540–1596). Two years later, no sign was found of the handful of men who were left behind to guard the settlement.

roman à clef

The French term ("novel with a key") denotes novels that camouflage real-life incidents and existing people under a layer of fiction. An example in American literature is Nathaniel Hawthorne's (1804–1864) *The Blithedale Romance* (1825), which uses the Brook Farm community of the transcendentalists as its thinly veiled setting and employs literary characters modeled on real-life people.

romance

Nathaniel Hawthorne's (1804–1864) definition of the literary genre of the romance assigns a central status to the imagination. From a modern perspective, there is hardly any difference between Hawthorne's romance and the traditional novel. For Hawthorne, however, the novel as it developed in the eighteenth century is characterized by a strong emphasis on realism, whereas the romance incorporates dreamlike, allegorical, and supernatural elements, thereby obscuring the borderline between imagination and reality.

romanticism

This movement in literary history in the first half of the nineteenth century is closely connected to the English poets Samuel Taylor Coleridge (1772–1834) and William Wordsworth (1770–1850). The "Preface" to *Lyrical Ballads* (1798) – a collection of poetry in which the two poets postulate a new poetic mode – is generally regarded as the beginning of a new era in literary history. Nature coupled with individual and emotional experiences, all of which are rendered in plain language, become key features. Romanticism may be seen as a reaction to the Enlightenment and the political changes throughout Europe and America at the end of the eighteenth century. In America, the movement of transcendentalism partly overlaps or shares features with romanticism.

Salem witchcraft trials

In this dark episode in the early history of New England in the 1690s, named after the city of Salem in colonial Massachusetts, numerous people were accused of witchcraft. The Puritan judges in these trials eventually found fourteen women and five men guilty of witchcraft and sentenced them to death by hanging. This early manifestation of mass hysteria in American cultural history inspired Arthur Miller (1915–2005) to write his play *The Crucible* (1953).

semiotics

Semiotics is the study of signs. This school in the second half of the twentieth century defined text as an interdependent network of signs. It expanded the notion of text to include nonverbal systems of signs, such as film, painting, fashion, or geography. Semiotics as an academic field builds on the concepts of language of the Swiss linguist Ferdinand de Saussure (1857–1913) and the American philosopher Charles Sanders Peirce (1839–1914).

sentimental novel

This subgenre of the novel in the late eighteenth century aimed at creating "sentiment," that is, compassion in the reader. It frequently portrays the fates of women, showing them in precarious situations created by male, often sexual, violence. Major American examples include William Hill Brown's (1765–1793) *The Power of Sympathy* (1789) and Hannah Foster's (1758–1840) *The Coquette; or, The History of Eliza Wharton* (1797).

signifier and signified

The Swiss linguist Ferdinand de Saussure (1857–1913) defined the linguistic sign as divided into two basic dimensions: the mental concept (e.g. the idea of a tree), termed the signified; and that concept's sound image (the sequence of sounds or letters, e.g. in the word "T-R-E-E"), termed the signifier.

slave narratives

Already in the eighteenth century, African Americans had raised their voices in personal narratives. These older texts, like Olaudah Equiano's (*c*.1745–1797) *The Interesting Narrative of the Life of Olaudah Equiano,* or *Gustavus Vassa, the African* (1789), focus mostly on the passage from the African homeland to the New World as well as the ensuing acculturation processes. Nineteenth-century authors, on the other hand, concentrate on the circumstances of a slave's individual everyday life and the chain of events leading to the person's emancipation from slavery. *Narrative of the Life of Frederick Douglass, an American Slave*, by the literate runaway slave Frederick Douglass (1818–1895), became an immediate bestseller after its publication in 1845. In a similar vein, Harriet Jacobs's (1813–1897) *Incidents in the Life of a Slave Girl* (1861) contributed to this growing African-American voice in autobiographies from a female perspective.

Southern Gothic

The term refers to a particular type of fiction, usually set in the US South, that is characterized by grotesque situations, derelict settings, and violent plots. Major authors include William Faulkner (1897–1962), Truman Capote (1924–1984), and Carson McCullers (1917–1967). Flannery O'Connor's (1925–1964) short story "A Good Man Is Hard to Find" (1953), with its absurd plot, a setting in the middle of nowhere, and its unmotivated violence, is a textbook example of Southern Gothic.

stream-of-consciousness technique

This narrative technique (related to interior monologue) is used to represent the subconscious associations of a literary character. It reflects a groundbreaking shift in cultural paradigms during the first decades of the twentieth century. The most famous example of a stream-of-consciousness technique is the final section of James Joyce's (1882–1941) English novel *Ulysses* (1922). In the 1930s, the American novelist John Dos Passos (1896–1970) in his trilogy *U.S.A.* (1930–1936) intersperses what he calls "camera-eye" passages throughout the novels in order to document the subjective point of view of an adolescent young man in the form of a stream-of-consciousness narration.

structuralism and formalism

These are general terms for text-oriented approaches in the twentieth century that use formal and structural aspects (intrinsic approach) in the interpretation of texts and neglect historical, sociological, biographical, and psychological dimensions. They try to find overarching, universal elements, rules, and structures within a certain genre or period of time. The most important schools are Russian formalism and the Prague school of structuralism in the first half of the twentieth century and French structuralism after World War II with its heyday in the 1960s. In the Anglo-American context, New Criticism developed as a related movement around World War II.

tales of ratiocination

These short stories are forerunners of the detective story. Edgar Allan Poe (1809–1849) coined this name for a particular subgenre of his short stories – for example, "The Murders in the Rue Morgue" (1841) – in which the reader or audience slips into the role of a detective who has to decipher the overall significance of certain aspects of the story. Because of their particular structure, the actual suspense of these tales lies in the correct way of reading the evidence, whereas solving the case becomes secondary.

tall tale

This term refers to a kind of cock-and-bull story, which is part of the folklore narratives of the American Southwest: an educated gentleman meets a clever local hero and the interaction between the two character types creates a situational comedy. Mark Twain's (1835–1910) early short stories and later novels rely heavily on this genre.

text-oriented approaches

This umbrella term refers to movements or schools in literary theory that concentrate on the "textual" or intrinsic levels of literature. They deliberately exclude extrinsic aspects (i.e. those external to the text) concerning the author (biography, complete works), audience (class, gender, age, ethnic origin, education), or context (historical, social, or political conditions). The text-oriented schools of the twentieth century include Russian formalism, the Prague school of structuralism, New Criticism, semiotics, and deconstruction.

theater of the absurd

This postmodernist movement in mid-twentieth-century drama abandons traditional plot structures and conventional character presentation in favor of new modes of portraying disillusionment in the human condition after World War II. Discontinuity of time and space, irrationality, breakdown of communication, meaninglessness, hopelessness, nonsense, and illogical structures are typical characteristics. The theater of the absurd is closely connected to the Irish playwright

Samuel Beckett (1906–1989) with his play *Waiting for Godot* (1952). Edward Albee's (1928–) adaptation of the theater of the absurd for an American context, especially in *The Zoo Story* (1958), becomes a milestone in American postmodern theater.

transcendentalism

Partly influenced by German idealism in philosophy and British literary romanticism of the late eighteenth century, American transcendentalism developed as one of the first indigenous literary and philosophical movements in the United States in the first half of the nineteenth century. Transcendentalism is causally connected to the American writer and philosopher Ralph Waldo Emerson (1803–1882), whose essays advocate a fresh and unobstructed approach to nature, which leaves behind the burden of traditional learning. The physical environment, or "nature" as the transcendentalists refer to it, becomes the prime object of philosophical inquiry, not as a goal in itself, but as a means of transcendence. Nature is the starting point for gaining a deeper understanding of the world at large. For the transcendentalists, intense sensual perception (= understanding) is used to arrive at a larger insight (= reason), which in turn serves as a stepping-stone to transcend these individual observations for a vision of the cosmic harmony in nature. To the inner circle of the movement belong Henry David Thoreau (1817–1862), Margaret Fuller (1810–1850), and to a certain extent Nathaniel Hawthorne (1804–1864). Influenced by transcendentalist ideas were Herman Melville's (1819–1891) novels, which revolve around the tension between the individual self and nature, as well as the poetry of Walt Whitman (1819–1892), which extends the transcendentalist concept of nature to the human body and all manifestations of American material culture.

unity of effect

Edgar Allan Poe (1809–1849), in his essay "The Philosophy of Composition" (1846), argues that all compositional elements in a text should work toward the common goal of achieving a "unity of effect" (273). For example, horror can function as a single overall effect. From this objective, Poe derives all ensuing steps of composition, such as the brevity of a text "to be read at one sitting" (273), or rhythmical and phonetic elements supporting the content level. In emphasizing the unity of a text, Poe anticipates one of the main tenets of the theoretical approaches of New Criticism in the middle of the twentieth century.

utopian literature

This subgenre of the novel describes alternative worlds with the aim of revealing and criticizing existing sociopolitical conditions. Although its origins go back to classical antiquity and the Middle Ages, the genre as such evolved in the early modern period with Thomas More's (1478–1535) *Utopia* (1515) under the influence of New World discoveries. The genre became very productive in the second half of the nineteenth century, partly influenced by numerous experimental or alternative communities throughout the United States. Major American utopian novels include Edward Bellamy's (1850–1898) *Looking Backward: 2000–1887* (1888), whose socioeconomic reflections exerted a major influence on subsequent social utopias, as did Charlotte Perkins Gilman's (1860–1935) *Herland* (1912) with respect to gender issues.

Virginia Company

King James I (1566–1625) divided the coastal areas between Canada and Florida into two regions, transferring the rights to collaborating investment groups that operated under the patronage of the so-called Virginia Company. The company system, which was made up of a number of contributing investors, replaced the older charter system under Queen Elizabeth I (1533–1603), which had granted only one individual, for example, Sir Walter Raleigh (*c*.1554–1618), the right to colonize a region.

Yale Critics

In the United States Jacques Derrida's (1930–2004) deconstruction was introduced and fostered by the Belgian literary theorist and Yale professor Paul de Man (1919–1983). The movement was soon taken up by the other Yale Critics, including Harold Bloom (1930–), Geoffrey Hartman (1929–), and J. Hillis Miller (1928–), who shaped the theoretical landscape in literary criticism of the 1980s. Similar to the way poststructuralism preserves structuralism while at the same time criticizing it, deconstruction built upon New Criticism and other formalist schools. Paul de Man, for example, rejected the notion of a single, correct interpretation of a text and instead tried to recover ambiguities and polysemies.

Suggested further reading

Primary texts

The following core reading list provides a cursory survey of the most important authors and texts in American literature. Although this list is only a crude reduction of the large number of important works in the history of American literature it might still be intimidating to the uninitiated reader. To make initial reading choices easier, the most representative texts for each period are underlined.

1. Discovery narratives

Christopher Columbus (1450/51–1506)
<u>Letter to Luis de Santangel Regarding the First Voyage (1493)</u>
Amerigo Vespucci (1452/54–1512)
Letter to Pier Soderini (1505/6)
Álvar Núñez Cabeza de Vaca (c.1490–c.1557)
La Relación (1542):
- Dedication
- The Malhado Way of Life
- Our Life among the Avavares and Arbadaos
- The First Confrontation

2. Colonial literature

Michele de Montaigne (1533–1592)
"Des Cannibales" (1580)
Thomas Harriot (c.1560–1621)
Brief and True Report of the New-Found Land of Virginia (1588):
- Chapter I

Thomas Morton (c.1579–1647)
  New English Canaan (1637):
  - Chapters XIV–XVI
John Smith (c.1580–1631)
  The General History of Virginia, New-England, and the Summer Isles (1624):
  - Third Book: What Happened till the First Supply
  - Fourth Book: Enquiry By King James
John Winthrop (1588–1649)
  <u>*A Model for Christian Charity* (1630)</u>
  Journal of John Winthrop/The History of New England, 1630–1649:
  - Arrival (June 8, 1630)
  - Charges against Roger Williams (December 27, 1633; January 11, 1636)
  - Charges against Anne Hutchinson (October 21, 1636; November 1, 1637; March 1638; March 22, 1638; September 1638; September 1643)
William Bradford (1590–1657)
  Of Plymouth Plantation (publ. 1856):
  - Chapters VIII–XII, XIX, XXXII
  <u>"Mayflower Compact" (1620)</u>
Richard Mather (1596–1669)
  Bay Psalm Book (1640):
  - "Psalm 23"
Roger Williams (1603–1683)
  A Key into the Language of America (1643):
  - Prefaces
  - Chapters I, II
Anne Bradstreet (c.1612–1672)
  The Tenth Muse Lately Sprung up in America (1650):
  - <u>"The Prologue"</u>
  - <u>"Verses upon the Burning of Our House, July 10th, 1666" (1678)</u>
  - "In Memory of My Dear Grandchild Elizabeth Bradstreet, Who Deceased August, 1665, Being a Year and a Half Old" (1678)
  - "The Author to Her Book" (1678)
Mary Rowlandson (c.1637–1678)
  A True History of the Captivity and Restoration of Mrs. Mary Rowlandson (1682)
Edward Taylor (1642–1729)
  <u>"Huswifery" (publ. 1939)</u>
  Preparatory Meditations (publ. 1939):
  - Prologue

- Meditation 8 from First Series
- Meditation 26 from Second Series

Cotton Mather (1663–1728)

The Wonders of the Invisible World (1693):
- A People of God in the Devil's Territories
- The Trial of Martha Carrier

Magnalia Christi Americana (1702):
- Galeacius Secundus: The Life of William Bradford, Esq., Governor of Plymouth Colony
- Nehemias Americanus: The Life of John Winthrop, Esq., Governor of Massachusetts Colony

Sarah Kemble Knight (1666–1727)

"The Journal of Madam Knight" (1825):
- Tuesday, October the Third

William Byrd (1674–1744)

The Secret Diary of Willam Byrd of Westover (1710–1712):
- December 31, 1710
- February 6, 1711

Anonymous

The New-England Primer (1687–1690):
- "Alphabet"

Jonathan Edwards (1703–1758)

"Sinners in the Hands of an Angry God" (1741)

"Personal Narrative" (publ. 1765)

Phillis Wheatley (1753–1784)

Poems on Various Subjects (1773):
- "On Being Brought from Africa to America"
- "To S. M., a Young African Painter, on Seeing His Works"

3. Literature of the Early Republic

Benjamin Franklin (1706–1790)

Poor Richard's Almanack (1732–1758)

The Autobiography of Benjamin Franklin (1771–1790)

J. Hector St. John de Crèvecoeur (1735–1813)

Letters from an American Farmer (1782):
- Letter III

Thomas Paine (1737–1809)

Common Sense (1776):
- Introduction
- Thoughts on the Present State of American Affairs

Thomas Jefferson (1743–1826)
> *The Declaration of Independence* (1776)
> *Notes on the State of Virginia* (1787):
> - Query VI (Indians of North America)

Olaudah Equiano (c.1745–1797)
> *The Interesting Narrative of the Life of Olaudah Equinano, or Gustavus Vassa, the African* (1789)

Hannah Webster Foster (1758–1826)
> *The Coquette or, The History of Eliza Wharton* (1797)

Tabitha Tenney (1762–1837)
> *Female Quixotism* (1801):
> - Book I: Chapters IX, XIV, XV

William Hill Brown (1765–1793)
> *The Power of Sympathy* (1789)

Charles Brockden Brown (1771–1810)
> *Edgar Huntly, Or, Memoirs of a Sleepwalker* (1799)

Washington Irving (1783–1859)
> *The Sketch Book of Geoffrey Crayon, Gent.* (1819/20):
> - "Rip van Winkle"
> - "The Legend of Sleepy Hollow"

James Fenimore Cooper (1789–1851)
> *The Last of the Mohicans* (1826):
> - Volume I: Chapter III

4. Transcendentalism

Ralph W. Emerson (1803–1882)
> *Nature* (1836)
> "The American Scholar" (1837)
> "Self-Reliance" (1841)
> "The Poet" (1844)

Nathaniel Hawthorne (1804–1864)
> "The May-Pole of Merry Mount" (1837)
> "The Birthmark" (1843/46)
> "Rapaccini's Daughter" (1844)
> *The Scarlet Letter* (1850)

Margaret Fuller (1810–1850)
> *Woman in the 19th Century* (1845):
> - "The Great Lawsuit: Man *versus* Men. Woman *versus* Women"

Henry D. Thoreau (1817–1862)
> "Resistance to Civil Government" (1849)
> *Walden* (1854)

5. American Renaissance

Sojourner Truth (1797–1883)
>"Speech to the Women's Rights Convention in Akron, Ohio, 1851" (1851)

Abraham Lincoln (1809–1865)
>*The Gettysburg Address* (1863)

Edgar Allan Poe (1809–1849)
>"Ligeia" (1838)
>"The Fall of the House of Usher" (1839)
>"The Murders in the Rue Morgue" (1841)
>"The Pit and the Pendulum" (1842)
>"The Conqueror Worm" (1843)
>"The Tell-Tale Heart" (1843)
>"The Raven" (1845)
>"The Philosophy of Composition" (1846)
>"Ulalume" (1847)
>"Annabel Lee" (1849)
>"The Bells" (1849)

Harriet Beecher Stowe (1811–1896)
>*Uncle Tom's Cabin* (1852):
>- Chapters I, III, VII, IX, XII–XIV, XX, XXX, XXXI, XXXIV, XL

Harriet Ann Jacobs (1813–1897)
>*Incidents in the Life of a Slave Girl* (1961):
>- Chapters I, VII, X, XIV, XXI, XLI

William Wells Brown (1815–1884)
>*Clotel; or The President's Daughter* (1853):
>- Chapters I, XXIV, XXV

Frederick Douglass (1818–1895)
>*Narrative of the Life of Frederick Douglass, an American Slave* (1845)

Herman Melville (1819–1891)
>*Typee* (1846)
>*Moby Dick* (1851):
>- Etymology
>- Chapters 1, 3, 4, 28, 36, 41, 42, 135
>- Epilogue
>
>"Bartleby, the Scrivener: A Story of Wall Street" (1856)
>"Billy Budd" (1886–1891)

Walt Whitman (1819–1892)
>*Leaves of Grass* (1855–1892):
>- "Preface" (1855)
>- "Song of Myself" (1855)

- "Crossing Brooklyn Ferry" (1856, 1881)
- "Spontaneous Me" (1856)
- "Out of the Cradle Endlessly Rocking" (1859, 1881)
- "From Pent-up Aching Rivers" (1860)
- "O Captain! My Captain!" (1865)
- "When Lilacs Last in the Dooryard Bloom'd" (1865/66, 1881)
- "One's Self I Sing" (1867, 1871)

Dion Boucicault (1820–1890)
The Octoroon (1859)

Maria Susanna Cummins (1827–1866)
The Lamplighter (1854)

Emily Dickinson (1830–1886)
"My Life had stood – a Loaded Gun" (1863)
"Because I could not stop for Death" (1890)
"I died for Beauty" (1890)
"I'm Nobody" (1891)
"I felt a Funeral, in my Brain" (1896)
"Over the fence" (1945)

6. Gilded Age – Realism

Rebecca Harding Davis (1831–1910)
Life in the Iron Mills (1861)

Louisa May Alcott (1832–1888)
Behind a Mask, or A Woman's Power (1866)

Mark Twain (1835–1910)
"The Celebrated Jumping Frog of Calaveras County" (1867)
The Adventures of Huckleberry Finn (1884)

William Dean Howells (1837–1920)
The Rise of Silas Lapham (1885)

Henry James (1843–1916)
Daisy Miller (1878)
The Portrait of a Lady (1881)
"The Beast in the Jungle" (1903)
"The Jolly Corner" (1908)

Edward Bellamy (1850–1898)
Looking Backward: 2000–1887 (1888)

Kate Chopin (1851–1904)
The Awakening (1899)

Charlotte Perkins Gilman (1860–1935)
"The Yellow Wallpaper" (1890)
Herland (1912)

Edith Wharton (1862–1937)
    <u>*The House of Mirth* (1905)</u>
Frank Norris (1870–1902)
    The Octopus: A Story of California (1901)
Stephen Crane (1871–1900)
    Maggie: A Girl of the Streets (1893)
    <u>*The Red Badge of Courage* (1895)</u>
Theodore Dreiser (1871–1945)
    Sister Carrie (1900)
Jack London (1876–1916)
    "To Build a Fire" (1902, 1908)
    The Call of the Wild (1903)

7. Modernism

Ambrose Bierce (1842–1914)
    <u>"An Occurrence at Owl Creek Bridge" (1890)</u>
Booker T. Washington (1856–1915)
    Up from Slavery (1901):
    - Chapters I, II, XIV
W. E. B. Du Bois (1868–1963)
    The Souls of Black Folk (1903):
    - The Forethought
    - Chapters I, III
Willa Cather (1873–1947)
    My Ántonia (1918)
Robert Frost (1874–1963)
    "Stars" (1913)
    "Mending Wall" (1914)
    "The Road Not Taken" (1916)
    <u>"Stopping by Woods on a Snowy Evening" (1920)</u>
Amy Lowell (1874–1925)
    "A Gift" (1914)
    "The Temple" (1914)
    "White and Green" (1914)
Gertrude Stein (1874–1946)
    Three Lives (1909):
    - "Melanctha" (1909)
    Tender Buttons (1914)
Susan Glaspell (1876–1948)
    <u>*Trifles* (1916)</u>

Wallace Stevens (1879–1955)
    "Le Monocle de Mon Oncle" (1918)
    "Anecdote of the Jar" (1919)
    "The Snow Man" (1931)
    "Not Ideas about the Thing but the Thing Itself" (1954)
William Carlos Williams (1883–1963)
    "The Uses of Poetry" (1909)
    "Portrait of a Lady" (1920, 1934)
    "Spring and All" (1923)
    "The Red Wheelbarrow" (1923)
    "This Is Just to Say" (1934)
Sinclair Lewis (1885–1951)
    Babbitt (1922)
Ezra Pound (1885–1972)
    "The Seafarer" (1911)
    "In a Station of the Metro" (1913)
    Cantos (1915–1962):
    - I, XVII, XLV, CXVI
    "A Retrospect" (1918)
Hilda Doolittle (H.D.) (1886–1961)
    "Pear Tree" (1916)
    "Leda" (1919, 1921)
    "Heat" (1922)
Marianne Moore (1887–1972)
    "The Fish" (1918, 1921)
    "Poetry" (1921, 1935)
    "A Grave" (1924)
T. S. Eliot (1888–1965)
    "The Love Song of J. Alfred Prufrock" (1915, 1917)
    "Hamlet and His Problems" (1919)
    "Gerontion" (1920)
    "Tradition and the Individual Talent" (1920)
    "The Metaphysical Poets" (1921)
    The Waste Land (1922)
    "Ash Wednesday" (1930)
Eugene O'Neill (1888–1953)
    Emperor Jones (1920)
    Long Day's Journey into Night (1956)
Katherine Anne Porter (1890–1980)
    "Old Mortality" (1937)

Zora Neale Hurston (1891–1960)
>   *Their Eyes Were Watching God* (1937)

Nella Larsen (1891–1964)
>   *Passing* (1929)

Thornton Wilder (1897–1975)
>   *Our Town* (1937)

Elmer Rice (1892–1967)
>   *The Adding Machine* (1923)

Hart Crane (1899–1932)
>   *The Bridge* (1930):
>   - The Brooklyn Bridge
>   - Powhatan's Daughter
>   - The Tunnel

e. e. cummings (1894–1962)
>   "next to of course god america i" (1926)
>   "un" (1938)
>   "love is more thicker than forget" (1940)
>   "pity this busy monster, manunkind" (1944)
>   "l(a" (1958)

Scott F. Fitzgerald (1896–1940)
>   *The Great Gatsby* (1925)
>   "Babylon Revisited" (1931)

John Dos Passos (1896–1970)
>   *The Big Money* (1936):
>   - Newsreel LXVIII
>   - The Camera Eye (51)
>   *Manhattan Transfer* (1925)

William Faulkner (1897–1962)
>   *The Sound and the Fury* (1929):
>   - April Seventh, 1828 (Benjy Section)
>   "A Rose for Emily" (1930)
>   *As I Lay Dying* (1930)
>   "Dry September" (1931)
>   *Light in August* (1932)

Ernest Hemingway (1899–1961)
>   "The Killers" (1927)
>   *The Sun also Rises* (1929)
>   *The Old Man and the Sea* (1951)

Langston Hughes (1902–1967)
>   "The Negro Speaks of Rivers" (1921)

"I, Too" (1925)
"Song for a Dark Girl" (1927)
"Freedom [1]" (1943)
"Words Like Freedom" (1943)
"Silhouette" (1944)
"Harlem" (1951)
John Steinbeck (1902–1968)
The Grapes of Wrath (1939)
Clifford Odets (1906–1963)
Waiting for Lefty (1935)
Lillian Hellman (1907–1984)
The Children's Hour (1934)
Tennessee Williams (1911–1983)
The Glass Menagerie (1944)
A Streetcar Named Desire (1947)
Arthur Miller (1915–2005)
Death of a Salesman (1949)
The Crucible (1953)

8. Postmodernism

Vladimir Nabokov (1899–1977)
Lolita (1955)
Pale Fire (1962)
Isaac Bashevis Singer (1902–1991)
"Gimpel the Fool" (1957)
Richard Wright (1908–1960)
Native Son (1940)
Ralph Ellison (1914–1994)
Invisible Man (1953)
Bernard Malamud (1914–1986)
"The Magic Barrel" (1958)
Saul Bellow (1915–2005)
Dangling Man (1944)
Herzog (1964)
Carson McCullers (1917–1967)
The Member of the Wedding (1946)
J. D. Salinger (1919–2010)
"A Perfect Day for Bananafish" (1948)
The Catcher in the Rye (1951)
Jack Kerouac (1922–1969)
On the Road (1951)

Suggested further reading

Kurt Vonnegut (1922–2007)
> *Slaughterhouse-Five* (1969)

Joseph Heller (1923–1999)
> *Catch-22* (1961)

Denise Levertov (1923–1997)
> "The Rights" (1957)
> "The Jacob's Ladder" (1961)
> "Advent 1966" (1971)

Norman Mailer (1923–)
> "The White Negro" (1957)
> *Armies of the Night* (1968)

James Baldwin (1924–1987)
> *Go Tell It on the Mountain* (1953)

Truman Capote (1924–1984)
> *Breakfast at Tiffany's* (1958)
> *In Cold Blood* (1966)

Flannery O'Connor (1925–1964)
> "A Good Man Is Hard to Find" (1953)
> "Everything that Rises Must Converge" (1965)

Allen Ginsberg (1926–1997)
> "A Supermarket in California" (1956)
> "An Asphodel" (1956)
> "Howl" (1956)

John Ashbery (1927–)
> *Self-Portrait in a Convex Mirror* (1975)

Edward Albee (1928–)
> *The Zoo Story* (1958)
> *Who's Afraid of Virginia Woolf?* (1962)

Raymond Federman (1928–2009)
> *Double or Nothing* (1971)

Ursula LeGuin (1929–)
> *The Left Hand of Darkness* (1969)

Adrienne Rich (1929–2012)
> "Aunt Jennifer's Tigers" (1951)
> "Living In Sin" (1954)
> "Miracle Ice Cream" (1995)

John Barth (1930–)
> "The Literature of Exhaustion" (1967)
> "Lost in the Funhouse" (1968)

Lorraine Hansberry (1930–1965)
> *A Raisin in the Sun* (1959)

Gary Snyder (1930–)
    "Riprap" (1959)
    "Civilization" (1970)
    "A Walk" (1971)
    "December At Yase" (1971)
    "Axe Handles" (1983)
Donald Barthelme (1931–1989)
    "At the End of the Mechanical Age" (1976)
Toni Morrison (1931–)
    Beloved (1987)
Robert Coover (1932–)
    "The Babysitter" (1969)
Sylvia Plath (1932–1963)
    "Edge" (1963)
    The Bell Jar (1963)
    "The Arrival of the Bee Box" (1965)
    "Tulips" (1965)
    "Daddy" (1966)
    "Lady Lazarus" (1966)
John Updike (1932–2009)
    Rabbit, Run (1960)
Philip Roth (1933–)
    Zuckermann Bound (1985)
LeRoi Jones (Amiri Baraka) (1934–)
    Dutchman (1964)
N. Scott Momaday (1934–)
    House Made of Dawn (1968)
Marge Piercy (1936–)
    Woman on the Edge of Time (1976)
Thomas Pynchon (1937–)
    The Crying of Lot 49 (1966)
Maxine Hong Kingston (1940–)
    The Woman Warrior (1975)
Luis Valdez (1940–)
    Los Vendidos (1967)
Sam Shepard (1943–)
    True West (1980)
    Fool for Love (1985)
Alice Walker (1944–)
    The Color Purple (1982)

David Mamet (1947–)
: *Sexual Perversity in Chicago* (1974)
: *Glengarry Glen Ross* (1984)

Paul Auster (1947–)
: *City of Glass* (1987)

Leslie Marmon Silko (1948–)
: *Ceremony* (1977)

Richard Price (1949–)
: *Clockers* (1995)

Jorie Graham (1950–)
: "The Way Things Work" (1980)
: "San Sepolcro" (1983)
: "Orpheus and Eurydice" (1987)

Amy Tan (1952–)
: *The Joy Luck Club* (1989)

Louise Erdrich (1954–)
: *Love Medicine* (1984, 1993, 2009)

Jonathan Franzen (1959–)
: *The Corrections* (2001)

David Foster Wallace (1962–2008)
: *Infinite Jest* (1997)

Bret Easton Ellis (1964–)
: *American Psycho* (1991)

Jonathan Safran Foer (1977–)
: *Extremely Loud and Incredibly Close* (2005)

Reference works

Primary text anthologies – general

Baym, Nina, et al., Eds. *The Norton Anthology of American Literature*. 8th ed. 5 vols. New York: Norton, 2011.

Lauter, Paul, et al., Eds. *The Heath Anthology of American Literature*. 7th ed. 5 vols. Boston, MA: Houghton Mifflin, 2013.

Primary text anthologies – specific

The American Revolution: Writings from the War of Independence. New York: Library of America, 2001.

Andrews, William L., Ed. *Slave Narratives*. New York: Library of America, 2000.

Beaty, Jerome, and J. Paul Hunter, Eds. *New Worlds of Literature: Writing from America's Many Cultures*. 2nd ed. New York: Norton, 1994.

Brunetti, Ivan, Ed. *An Anthology of Graphic Fiction, Cartoons, and True Stories*. New Haven, NJ: Yale University Press, 2006.

Castillo, Susan P., and Ivy T. Schweitzer, Eds. *The Literatures of Colonial America: An Anthology*. Malden, MA: Blackwell, 2001.

Gates, Henry Louis, Jr., Ed. *The Norton Anthology of African American Literature*. 2nd ed. New York: Norton, 2003.

Gilbert, Sandra M., and Susan D. Gubar, Eds. *The Norton Anthology of Literature by Women: The Traditions in English*. 2nd ed. New York: Norton, 1996.

Gunn, Giles, Ed. *Early American Writing*. New York: Penguin, 1994.

Hill, Patricia L., et al., Eds. *Call and Response: The Riverside Anthology of the African American Literary Tradition*. New York: Houghton, 1998.

Jehlen, Myra, and Michael Warner, Eds. *The English Literatures of America, 1500–1800*. New York: Routledge, 1997.

Kanellos, Nicolas, et al., Eds. *Herencia: The Anthology of Hispanic Literature of the United States*. New York: Oxford University Press, 2002.

Lentricchia, Frank, Ed. *The Norton Anthology of Theory and Criticism*. New York: Norton, 2001.

Lim, Shirley G., Ed. *Asian-American Literature: An Anthology*. Lincolnwood, IL: NTC, 2005.

Sayre, Robert F., Ed. *American Lives: An Anthology of Autobiographical Writing*. Madison, WI: University of Wisconsin Press, 1994.

Sollors, Werner, Ed. *An Anthology of Interracial Literature*. New York: New York University Press, 2004.

Sollors, Werner, and Marc Shell, Eds. *Multilingual Anthology of American Literature*. New York: New York University Press, 2000.

Trout, Lawana, Ed. *Native American Literature: An Anthology*. Lincolnwood, IL: NTC, 1999.

Turner, Frederick, Ed. *The Portable North American Indian Reader*. New York: Penguin, 1974.

Literary histories

Bercovitch, Sacvan, Ed. *The Cambridge History of American Literature*. 7 vols. New York: Cambridge University Press, 1994–2005.

Elliott, Emory, Ed. *Columbia Literary History of the United States*. New York: Columbia University Press, 1988.

Gray, Richard. *A History of American Literature*. 2nd ed. New York: Blackwell, 2011.

Hall, David D., Ed. *A History of the Book in America*. 5 vols. Chapel Hill, NC: University of North Carolina Press, 2007–2010.

Spiller, Robert, et al., Eds. *A Literary History of the United States*. 4th ed. New York: Macmillan, 1974.

Handbooks

Andrews, William L., et al., Eds. *The Concise Oxford Companion to African American Literature*. New York: Oxford University Press, 2001.

Davidson, Cathy, et al., Eds. *The Oxford Companion to Women's Writing in the United States*. New York: Oxford University Press, 1995.

Hart, James D., Ed. *The Oxford Companion to American Literature*. 6th ed. New York: Oxford University Press, 1995.

Nelson, Cary, Ed. *The Oxford Handbook of Modern and Contemporary American Poetry*. Oxford: Oxford University Press, 2012.

Nelson, Emmanuel S., Ed. *The Greenwood Encyclopedia of Multiethnic American Literature*. 5 vols. Westport, CT: Greenwood, 2005.

Ostrom, Hans, and J. David Macey, Eds. *The Greenwood Encyclopedia of African American Literature*. 5 vols. Westport, CT: Greenwood, 2005.

Serafin, Steven R., et al., Eds. *The Continuum Encyclopedia of American Literature*. New York: Continuum, 2003.

Standard works on particular aspects of American literature

Bercovitch, Sacvan. *The Puritan Origins of the American Self: With a New Preface*. 1975. New Haven, CT: Yale University Press, 2011.

Coronado, Raúl. *A World Not to Come: A History of Latino Writing and Print Culture*. Cambridge, MA: Harvard University Press, 2013.

Davidson, Cathy N. *Revolution and the Word: The Rise of the Novel in America.* 1986. New York: Oxford University Press, 2004.

Ernest, John. *Liberation Historiography: African American Writers and the Challenge of History, 1749–1861.* Chapel Hill, NC: University of North Carolina Press, 2004.

Fiedler, Leslie A. *Love and Death in the American Novel.* 1957/60. Normal, IL: Dalkey Archive, 2003.

Gates, Henry Louis, Jr. *The Signifying Monkey: A Theory of African-American Literary Criticism.* New York: Oxford University Press, 1988.

Greeson, Jennifer. *Our South: Geographic Fantasy and the Rise of National Literature.* Cambridge, MA: Harvard University Press, 2010.

Kolodny, Annett. *The Lay of the Land: Metaphor as Experience and History in American Life and Letters.* Chapel Hill, NC: University of North Carolina Press, 1975.

Lawrence, D. H. *Studies in Classic American Literature.* 1923. Eds. Ezra Greenspan et al. Cambridge: Cambridge University Press, 2003.

Lewis, R. W. B. *The American Adam: Innocence, Tragedy, and Tradition in the Nineteenth Century.* 1959. Chicago, IL: Chicago University Press, 1995.

Marx, Leo. *The Machine in the Garden: Technology and the Pastoral Ideal in America.* 1964. London: Oxford University Press, 2000.

Matthiessen, F. O. *American Renaissance: Art and Expression in the Age of Emerson and Whitman.* 1941. London: Oxford University Press, 1968.

Miller, Perry. *Errand into the Wilderness.* Cambridge, MA: Harvard University Press, 1956.

Parrington, Vernon Louis. *Main Currents in American Thought: An Interpretation of American Literature from the Beginnings to 1920.* 1927/30. 3 vols. Whitefish, MT: Kessinger, 2005.

Rubin, Joan S. *Songs of Ourselves: The Uses of Poetry in America.* Cambridge, MA: Belknap Press of Harvard University Press, 2007.

Smith, Henry Nash. *Virgin Land: The American West as Symbol and Myth.* 1950. Cambridge: Cambridge University Press, 2000.

Sundquist, Eric J. *To Wake the Nations: Race in the Making of American Literature.* Cambridge, MA: Harvard University Press, 1993.

Bibliography

Bierce, Ambrose. "An Occurrrence at Owl Creek Bridge." *The Complete Short Stories of Ambrose Bierce*. Ed. Ernest Jerome Hopkins. Lincoln, NE: University of Nebraska Press, 1984. 305–313.

Bradford, William. *Of Plymouth Plantation, 1620–1647*. Ed. Samuel E. Morison. New York: Knopf, 1959.

Bradstreet, Anne. "Here Follows Some Verses upon the Burning of Our House, July 10th, 1666." *The Works of Anne Bradstreet in Prose and Verse*. Ed. John Harvard Ellis. Gloucester, MA: Peter Smith, 1962. 40–42.

——. "In Memory of My Dear Grandchild Elizabeth Bradstreet, Who Deceased August, 1665, Being a Year and a Half Old." *The Works of Anne Bradstreet in Prose and Verse*. Ed. John Harvard Ellis. Gloucester, MA: Peter Smith, 1962. 404.

——. "The Prologue." *The Works of Anne Bradstreet in Prose and Verse*. Ed. John Harvard Ellis. Gloucester, MA: Peter Smith, 1962. 100–102.

Brown, Charles Brockden. "To the Public." *Edgar Huntly, Or, Memoirs of a Sleepwalker*. Port Washington, NY: Kennikat, 1963. 3–4.

Crane, Hart. "The Bridge." *The Complete Poems and Selected Letters and Prose of Hart Crane*. Ed. Brom Weber. London: Oxford University Press, 1968.

cummings, e. e. "l(a." *Complete Poems, 1904–1962*. Ed. George F. Firmage. New York: Liveright, 1991. 673.

Dickinson, Emily. "I Felt a Funeral, in My Brain." *The Poems of Emily Dickinson*. Ed. R. W. Franklin. Cambridge, MA: Belknap Press of Harvard University Press, 1998. 365–366.

——. "My Life had stood – a Loaded Gun." *The Poems of Emily Dickinson*. Ed. R. W. Franklin. Cambridge, MA: Belknap Press of Harvard University Press, 1998. 722–723.

——. "Over the fence." *The Poems of Emily Dickinson*. Ed. R. W. Franklin. Cambridge, MA: Belknap Press of Harvard University Press, 1998. 289.

Edwards, Jonathan. "Personal Narrative." *Basic Writings*. Ed. Ola Elizabeth Winslow. New York: Meridian, 1987. 81–96.

———. "Sinners in the Hands of an Angry God." *Basic Writings*. Ed. Ola Elizabeth Winslow. New York: Meridian, 1987. 150–167.

Eliot, T. S. "Hamlet and His Problems." *Selected Essays*. London: Faber and Faber, 1969. 141–146.

Emerson, Ralph Waldo. "The American Scholar." *Essays and Lectures*. Ed. Joel Porte. New York: Literary Classics of the United States, 1983. 51–71.

———. "Letter to Walt Whitman, July 21, 1855." *Leaves of Grass: The First (1855) Edition*. Ed. Malcolm Cowley. London: Secker and Warburg, 1960. ix.

———. "Nature." *Essays and Lectures*. Ed. Joel Porte. New York: Literary Classics of the United States, 1983. 5–49.

Faulkner, William. *The Sound and the Fury*. Harmondsworth, UK: Penguin, 1978.

Frost, Robert. "Stopping by Woods on a Snowy Evening." *The Poems of Robert Frost*. New York: Random House, 1946. 238.

Gilman, Charlotte Perkins. *The Home: Its Work and Influence*. Walnut Creek, CA: Rowman Altamira, 2002.

Ginsberg, Allen. "Howl." *Howl and Other Poems*. San Francisco, CA: City Light, 1959. 9–26.

Hemingway, Ernest. "The Killers." *The Essential Hemingway*. Harmondsworth, UK: Penguin, 1971. 378–387.

Irving, Washington. "Rip Van Winkle." *The Complete Works of Washington Irving in One Volume: With a Memoir of the Author*. Paris: Baudry's European Library, 1843. 233–240.

James, Henry. "The Jolly Corner." *The American Novels and Stories of Henry James*. Ed. F. O. Matthiessen. New York: Knopf, 1956. 792–819.

Jefferson, Thomas. *Autobiography of Thomas Jefferson*. New York: Capricorn, 1959.

London, Jack. *The Call of the Wild*. New York: Macmillan, 1903.

Mather, Cotton, Increase Mather, and Deodat Lawson. *The Wonders of the Invisible World: Being an Account of the Tryals of Several Witches Lately Executed in New England*. London: John Russell Smith, 1862.

Melville, Herman. "Bartleby, the Scrivener." *Billy Budd, Sailor and Other Stories*. London: Penguin, 1985. 57–99.

———. *Moby Dick*. London: Penguin, 1994.

———. *Typee: A Peep at Polynesian Life*. Harmondsworth, UK: Penguin, 1981.

Poe, Edgar Allan. "The Philosophy of Composition." *Poems and Essays*. Ed. John H. Ingram. Leipzig: Bernhard Tauchnitz, 1884. 270–286.

Pound, Ezra. "CXVI." *The Cantos of Ezra Pound*. London: New Directions, 1989. 815–817.

———. "In a Station of the Metro." *Selected Poems*. Ed. T. S. Eliot. London: Faber and Faber, 1967. 113.

———. "A Retrospect." *Literary Essays of Ezra Pound*. Ed. T. S. Eliot. London: Faber and Faber, 1963. 3–14.

Shakespeare, William. *Macbeth*. Ed. Kenneth Muir. London: Methuen, 1962.

Smith, John. *Captain John Smith's America: Selections from His Writings*. Ed. John Lankford. New York: Harper and Row, 1967.

St. John de Crèvecoeur, J. Hector. *Letters from an American Farmer*. New York: E. P. Dutton, 1957.

Stein, Gertrude. "Melanctha." *Three Lives*. Harmondsworth, UK: Penguin, 1990. 57–167.

Stevens, Wallace. "Anecdote of the Jar." *Selected Poems*. London: Faber and Faber, 1976. 36.

Taylor, Edward. "Huswifery." *The Poetical Works of Edward Taylor*. Ed. Thomas H. Johnson. Princeton, NJ: Princeton University Press, 1974. 116.

Thoreau, Henry David. "Civil Disobedience." *Walden and Civil Disobedience*. New York: Penguin, 1983. 383–413.

———. "Walden." *Walden and Civil Disobedience*. New York: Penguin, 1983. 43–382.

Vespucci, Amerigo. "The Four Voyages of Amerigo Vespucci." *Cosmographiae Introductio by Martin Waldseemüller and the English Translation of Joseph Fischer and Franz von Wieser (1507)*. Ann Arbor, MI: University Microfilm, 1966. 83–151.

Vonnegut, Kurt. *Slaughterhouse-Five*. London: Triad Paladin Grafton, 1989.

Wheatley, Phillis. "On Being Brought from Africa to America." *The Collected Works of Phillis Wheatley*. Ed. John Shields. New York: Oxford University Press, 1989. 18.

Whitman, Walt. "From Pent-Up Aching Rivers." *The Poetry and Prose of Walt Whitman*. Ed. Louis Untermeyer. New York: Simon and Schuster, 1949. 144–146.

———. "Preface." *Leaves of Grass: The First (1855) Edition*. Ed. Malcolm Cowley. London: Secker and Warburg, 1960. 5–24.

———. "Song of Myself." *The Poetry and Prose of Walt Whitman*. Ed. Louis Untermeyer. New York: Simon and Schuster, 1949. 95–143.

———. "Spontaneous Me." *The Poetry and Prose of Walt Whitman*. Ed. Louis Untermeyer. New York: Simon and Schuster, 1949. 154–155.

Williams, William Carlos. "The Red Wheelbarrow." *The Collected Earlier Poems*. New York: New Directions, 1966. 277.

Winthrop, John. "A Model of Christian Charity." *The Journal of John Winthrop, 1630–1649*. Ed. Richard S. Dunn and Laetitia Yeandle. Cambridge, MA: Harvard University Press, 1996. 1–11.

Author and title index

1919 (1932) 87
42nd Parallel, The (1930) 87

Adams, Henry (1838–1918) 134
Adding Machine, The (1923) 83–84, 141
Adorno, Theodor W. (1903–1969) 126, 143
Adventures of Huckleberry Finn, The (1884) 61–63, 143
Aeneid (29–19 BC) 21
Albee, Edward (1928–) 93–94, 153, 160
Alcott, Amos Bronson (1799–1888) 37, 67
Alcott, Louisa May (1832–1888) 67
Altman, Robert (1925–2006) 95
American Dictionary of the English Language (1828) 28
American Psycho (1991) 104
"American Scholar, The" (1837) 38
Anatomy of Criticism (1957) 116, 133
"Anecdote of the Jar" (1919) 77
Antonioni, Michelangelo (1912–2007) 95
Anxiety of Influence, The (1973) 116
As I Lay Dying (1930) 88
Ashbery, John (1927–) 96, 153

Arnold, Matthew (1822–1888) 112
"Art of Fiction, The" (1884) 113
Atlantic Monthly (1857–) 64, 113
Auster, Paul (1947–) 103–104, 146, 153
Autobiography of Benjamin Franklin, The (1771–1790) 29–30, 40, 47, 134
Awakening, The (1899) 67

Babbitt, Irving (1865–1933) 114, 119, 151
Baldwin, James (1924–1987) 106, 132
Barthes, Roland (1915–1980) 115, 122
"Bartleby, the Scrivener: A Story of Wall Street" (1856) 46
Barth, John (1930–) 103, 153
Baudelaire, Charles (1821–1867) 50
Bay Psalm Book (1640) 19
Beckett, Samuel (1906–1989) 93, 160
Behind a Mask (1866) 67
Bell Jar, The (1963) 98
Bellamy, Edward (1850–1898) 69, 161
Bellow, Saul (1915–2005) 108, 146

Beloved (1987) 106
Bhabha, Homi K. (1949–) 128, 152
Bierce, Ambrose (1842–1913) 70–71, 148
Big Money, The (1936) 87
Blithedale Romance, The (1852) 43, 156
Bloom, Harold (1930–) 116, 124, 161
Boccaccio, Giovanni (1313–1375) 75
Bordwell, David (1947–) 123, 142
Borges, Jorge Luis (1899–1986) 103
Boucicault, Dion (1820–1890) 51
Bradford, William (1590–1657) 14, 17, 136, 147, 152
Bradstreet, Anne (*c.*1612–1672) 20–22, 112, 136
Brando, Marlon (1924–2004) 91
Brecht, Bertolt (1898–1856) 91, 133
Brendan of Clonfert (*c.*484–*c.*577 AD) 1
Bridge, The (1930) 80
Brief and True Report of the New-Found Land of Virginia (1588) 10
Brooks, Gwendolyn (1917–2000) 132
Brown, Charles Brockden (1771–1810) 32–33, 48, 112, 139, 144
Brown, William Hill (1765–1793) 31, 139, 157
Burckhardt, Jacob (1818–1897) 127
Burke, Edmund (1729–1797) 32
Butler, Judith (1956–) 130, 143
Byrd, William (1674–1744) 26

Cabeza de Vaca, Álvar Núñez (*c.*1490–*c.*1557) 6
Cabot, John (*c.*1450–1498) 7

Call of the Wild, The (1903) 63
Calvin, John (1509–1564) 15, 153
"Cannibales, Des" (1580) 13
Cantos (1915–1962) 74–75, 140
Capote, Truman (1924–1984) 104, 158
Carnegie, Andrew (1835–1919) 60
Carrier, Martha (d. 1692) 20
Cartier, Jacques (1491–1557) 7
Castillo, Ana (1953–) 107, 135
Castle of Otranto, The (1764) 32
Catch-22 (1961) 103
Catcher in the Rye, The (1951) 99
Celebrated Jumping Frog of Calaveras County, The (1867) 61
Ceremony (1977) 107, 150
Cervantes, Miguel de (1547–1616) 32, 148, 151
Cézanne, Paul (1839–1906) 72
Champlain, Samuel de (1567–1635) 7–8
Chatman, Seymour (1928–) 123, 143
Children's Hour, The (1934) 91
Chopin, Kate (1851–1904) 67
Cisneros, Sandra (1954–) 107, 135
Civilization of the Renaissance in Italy, The (1860) 127
Cixous, Hélène (1937–) 130
Clarel: A Poem and Pilgrimage in the Holy Land (1876) 140
Clarissa (1748) 31
Clockers (1995) 108
Coleridge, Samuel Taylor (1772–1834) 34, 37, 156
Color Purple, The (1982) 106
Columbus, Christopher (1451–1506) 1–2, 6–7, 139
Common Sense (1776) 28
Conrad, Joseph (1857–1924) 85

Cooper, James Fenimore
  (1789–1851) 35–36, 139
Coquette, The (1797) 31, 140, 157
Corrections, The (2001) 104
Cortés, Hernán (1485–1547) 6
Count of Monte Cristo, The
  (1844–1846) 81
Crane, Hart (1899–1932) 80
Crane, Stephen (1871–1900) 66,
  103, 150
Creeley, Robert (1926–2005) 96,
  135
Criticism and Fiction (1891) 64, 113,
  155
Cromwell, Oliver (1599–1658) 155
Crucible, The (1953) 20, 92, 147, 157
Crying of Lot 49, The (1966) 101,
  103
Culture and Society (1958) 127, 137
cummings, e. e. (1894–1962) 58, 76,
  79–80, 136
Cummins, Maria Susanna
  (1827–1866) 50

da Verrazano, Giovanni
  (1485–1528) 7
Daisy Miller (1878) 64
Dangling Man (1944) 108
Dante Alighieri (*c.*1265–1321) 75,
  80, 140
David Copperfield (1850) 99
de Bry, Theodor (1528–1598) 9
de Gouges, Olympe (1748–1793)
  41, 141
de Man, Paul (1919–1983) 124–125,
  130, 138, 161
de Soto, Hernando (1496 or
  1500–1542) 6
Death of a Salesman (1949) 92, 95
"Death of the Author, The" (1968)
  103, 115

Declaration of Independence (1776) 29,
  41, 137–138, 140
Derrida, Jacques (1930–2004) 103,
  123–124, 130, 138, 161
Dexter (2006–2013) 104, 108
Dial (1840–1929) 38
Dickens, Charles (1812–1870) 99
Dickinson, Emily (1830–1886)
  56–60
Dissertation on the English Language
  (1789) 28
Doolittle, Hilda (1886–1961) 76,
  145
Donne, John (1572–1631) 148
Don Quijote (1605, 1615) 32, 148,
  151
Dos Passos, John (1896–1970) 87,
  103, 149, 158
Dostoyevsky, Fyodor (1821–1881)
  97
Double or Nothing (1971) 101
Douglass, Frederick (1818–1895) 52,
  132, 134, 158
Drake, Francis (*c.*1540–1596) 11,
  156
Dreiser, Theodore (1871–1945) 67,
  85, 150
Dryden, John (1631–1700) 112
Du Bois, W. E. B. (1868–1963) 84,
  132, 145
Duncan, Isadora (1877–1927) 87
Dutchman (1964) 94

Eco, Umberto (1932–) 122
Edgar Huntly (1799) 33, 48, 113,
  144
Education of Henry Adams, The
  (1918) 134
Edwards, Jonathan (1703–1758)
  23–24, 136, 144–145
Eisenstein, Sergei (1898–1948) 142

Eliot, T. S. (1888–1965) 59, 73, 75–80, 85, 100, 114, 145, 149, 151, 154
Elizabeth I of England (1533–1603) 9–10, 156, 161
Ellis, Bret Easton (1964–) 104
Ellison, Ralph (1914–1994) 96
Emerson, Ralph Waldo (1803–1882) 37–41, 44, 50, 52, 54–56, 61, 113, 160
Emperor Jones, The (1920) 81–82, 141
Empson, William (1906–1984) 119
Equiano, Olaudah (c.1745–1797) 51–52, 132, 134, 157
Essay Concerning Human Understanding, An (1690) 24
Extremely Loud and Incredibly Close (2003) 108

Faulkner, William (1897–1962) 62, 88–89, 110, 149, 158
Federman, Raymond (1928–2009) 101
Female Quixotism (1801) 32, 152
Feminine Mystique, The (1963) 129
Ferlinghetti, Lawrence (1919–) 95–96, 134
Film Language (1974) 122, 142
Fish, Stanley (1938–) 119
Fitzgerald, F. Scott (1896–1940) 73, 85, 87, 146
Fitzgerald, Zelda (1900–1948) 85
Flaubert, Gustave (1821–1880) 64
Foer, Jonathan Safran (1977–) 108, 146
Fool for Love (1985) 95
Ford, Henry (1863–1947) 87
Forerunner (1909–1916) 69
Foster, Hannah (1758–1840) 31

Franklin, Benjamin (1706–1790) 28–30, 39–40, 47, 134, 137, 140
Franzen, Jonathan (1959–) 104
Freud, Sigmund (1856–1939) 71, 116, 149, 153–154
Friedan, Betty (1921–2006) 129, 141
Frobisher, Martin (c.1535–1594) 9
"From Pent-up Aching Rivers" (1860) 55
Frost, Robert (1874–1963) 76–77
Frye, Northrop (1912–1991) 116, 133
Fuller, Margaret (1810–1850) 37, 41, 43, 129, 141, 165

Galle, Theodor (1571–1633) 3
Gandhi, Mahatma (1869–1948) 40
Gass, William (1924–) 103, 148
Gates, Henry Louis (1959–) 128
Geertz, Clifford (1926–2006) 128
Gender Trouble (1990) 130
General History of Virginia, New-England, and the Summer Isles, The (1624) 12–13
Gettysburg Address (1863) 138
Gilman, Charlotte Perkins (1860–1935) 41, 68–69, 83, 98, 129, 141, 161
"Gimpel the Fool" (1957) 108
Ginsberg, Allen (1926–1997) 55, 95, 134
Giovanni, Nikki (1943–) 132
Glaspell, Susan (1876–1948) 82–83
Glass Menagerie, The (1944) 91
Glengarry Glen Ross (1984) 94
Go Tell It on the Mountain (1953) 106
"Good Man Is Hard to Find, A" (1953) 98, 158
Gramsci, Antonio (1891–1937) 126

Author and title index 185

Grapes of Wrath, The (1939) 90
Great Gatsby, The (1925) 46, 85, 87, 146
Green Grow the Lilacs (1931) 149
Greenblatt, Stephen (1943–) 127, 150

Habermas, Jürgen (1929–) 126, 143
"Hamlet and His Problems" (1919) 75, 151
Hansberry, Lorraine (1930–1965) 94, 132
Harpers' Magazine (1850–) 105, 113
Harriot, Thomas (*c.*1560–1621) 10–11, 127
Hartman, Geoffrey (1929–) 124, 161
Hawthorne, Nathaniel (1804–1864) 17, 37, 41–46, 64, 113, 156, 160
Heart of Darkness (1902) 85
Helen in Egypt (1952–1954) 76
Heller, Joseph (1923–1999) 103
Hellman, Lillian (1905–1984) 91
Hemingway, Ernest (1898–1961) 73, 89–90
Henry VII of England (1457–1509) 7, 9
Herbert, George (1593–1633) 148
Herland (1912) 69, 161
Herzog (1964) 108
History of New York, A (1809) 34
Hitchcock, Alfred (1899–1980) 117
Hoffmann, E. T. A. (1776–1822) 48, 116
Home: Its Work and Influence, The (1903) 68
Homer (*c.* seventh century BC) 75, 140
House Made of Dawn (1968) 107, 149

House of Mirth, The (1905) 69
Howells, William Dean (1837–1920) 63–64, 113–114, 155
"Howl" (1956) 95–96
Hughes, Langston (1902–1967) 84, 132, 145
Hurston, Zora Neale (1891–1960) 84, 132, 145
"Huswifery" (publ. 1939) 22, 136
Hutchinson, Anne (1591–1643) 15, 19

Ibsen, Henrik (1828–1906) 94
"I Have a Dream" (1963) 138
"I felt a Funeral, in my Brain" (publ. 1896) 57
Iliad (*c.* seventh century BC) 80
Imitation of Life (1934) 85
"In a Station of the Metro" (1913) 74, 144
In Cold Blood (1966) 104
"In Memory of My Dear Grandchild Elizabeth Bradstreet, Who Deceased August, 1665, Being a Year and a Half Old" (publ. 1678) 22
Inception (2010) 71
Incidents in the Life of a Slave Girl (1861) 52, 158
Infinite Jest (1997) 104
Inglourious Basterds (2009) 98
Interesting Narrative of the Life of Olaudah Equiano, or Gustavus Vassa, the African, The (1789) 51, 157
Invisible Man (1953) 96–97, 106
Irigaray, Luce (1932–) 130
Irving, Washington (1783–1859) 34–35, 139
Iser, Wolfgang (1926–2007) 118, 145, 155

Jacobs, Harriet (1813–1897) 52, 132, 134, 158
James I of England (1566–1625) 12, 161
James, Henry (1843–1916) 64–67, 69, 88, 90, 113–114, 142, 150, 155
Jameson, Fredric (1934–) 126
Jefferson, Thomas (1743–1826) 29, 34, 137, 140
Johnson, Samuel (1709–1784) 148
"Jolly Corner, The" (1908) 66
Jones, LeRoi / Amiri Baraka (1934–) 94, 132, 153
Journal of John Winthrop / The History of New England from 1630–1649 (1790, 1825, 1826) 18
Journal of Richard Mather (publ. 1850) 19
Joy Luck Club, The (1989) 108
Joyce, James (1882–1941) 98, 158
Jung, C. G. (1875–1961) 81, 116, 133, 149, 154

Keats, John (1795–1821) 78
Kerouac, Jack (1922–1969) 95, 134
Key into the Language of America, A (1643) 15
"Killers, The" (1927) 89
King, Martin Luther, Jr. (1929–1968) 40, 94, 138
Kingston, Maxine Hong (1940–) 108, 133
Knight, Sarah Kemble (1666–1727) 26
Kracauer, Siegfried (1889–1966) 142
Kristeva, Julia (1941–) 130

"l(a" (1958) 79
Lacan, Jacques (1901–1981) 103, 117, 153–154

Lamplighter, The (1854) 50
Larsen, Nella (1891–1964) 84, 145
Last of the Mohicans, The (1826) 35
Leatherstocking Tales (1823–1841) 35
Leaves of Grass (1855) 52–54, 113
Lee, Spike (1957–) 108
"Legend of Sleepy Hollow, The" (1819–1820) 34
Letters from an American Farmer (1782) 27
Levertov, Denise (1923–1997) 96, 135
Life and Voyages of Christopher Columbus, The (1828) 34
"Ligeia" (1838) 49
Lincoln, Abraham (1809–1865) 50, 138
Literature and the American College (1908) 114, 151
"Literature of Exhaustion, The" (1967) 103
Literature of Their Own, A (1977) 129
Location of Culture, The (1994) 128, 152
Locke, Alain (1885–1954) 84, 145
Locke, John (1632–1704) 24, 28, 139
Lolita (1955) 100
London, Jack (1876–1916) 63
Long Day's Journey into Night (c.1941; publ. 1956) 115
Looking Backward: 2000–1887 (1888) 69
Lorca, Federico García (1898–1936) 55
Lowell, James Russell (1819–1891) 61
Lukács, Georg (1885–1971) 126
Lynch, David (1946–) 101
Lyotard, Jean-François (1924–1998) 153

Machine in the Garden, The (1964) 116, 133
Mad Men (2007–) 108
Maggie: A Girl of the Streets (1893) 66, 150
Magic Barrel, The (1958) 108
Magnalia Christi Americana (1702) 19
Mailer, Norman (1923–2007) 146
Malamud, Bernard (1914–1986) 108, 146
Malcolm X (1925–1965) 94
Mallarmé, Stéphane (1842–1898) 50
Mamet, David (1947–) 94
Marvell, Andrew (1621–1678) 148
Marx, Karl (1818–1883) 126, 147
Marx, Leo (1919–) 116, 133
*M*A*S*H* (1972–1983) 103
Mather, Cotton (1663–1728) 19–20, 136
Mather, Increase (1639–1723) 19
Mather, Richard (1596–1669) 19
Matthiessen, F. O. (1902–1950) 44, 133
"Mayflower Compact" (1620) 14, 147
"May-Pole of Merry Mount, The" (1837) 17, 42
McCarthy, Joseph (1908–1957) 20, 92, 147
McCullers, Carson (1917–1967) 98, 158
McTeague (1899) 67
"Melanctha" (1909) 72, 84
Mellon, Thomas (1813–1908) 60
Melville, Herman (1819–1891) 44–47, 55, 85, 140, 143, 160
Member of the Wedding, The (1946) 98
Memoirs of Margaret Fuller Ossoli (1852) 41

Metamorphoses (1 BC–AD 10) 2
"Metaphysical Poets, The" (1921) 75
Metz, Christian (1931–1993) 122, 142
Micheaux, Oscar (1884–1951) 85, 145
Miller, Arthur (1915–2005) 20, 92, 95, 147, 157
Miller, J. Hillis (1928–) 124, 161
Milton, John (1608–1674) 119
Moby Dick (1851) 45–46, 85, 143
Model for Christian Charity, A (1630) 18, 145
Momaday, N. Scott (1934–) 107, 149
Montaigne, Michele de (1533–1592) 13, 151
Moore, Marianne (1887–1972) 76
More, Thomas (1478–1535) 139, 161
Morrison, Toni (1931–) 106, 132
Morton, Thomas (c.1579–1647) 17, 42
Mulvey, Laura (1941–) 117, 142
Münsterberg, Hugo (1863–1916) 117, 142
"Murders in the Rue Morgue, The" (1841) 48–49, 119, 159
Mussolini, Benito (1883–1945) 74, 125
"My Life had stood – a Loaded Gun" (publ. 1863) 56–58

Nabokov, Vladimir (1899–1977) 99–100, 104, 153–154
Name of the Rose, The (1980) 122
Nänny, Max (1932–2006) 90
Narration in the Fiction Film (1985) 123

Narrative of the Life of Frederick Douglass, an American Slave (1845) 52, 158
Native Son (1940) 106
Nature (1836) 37–38
New English Canaan (1637) 17
New Negro, The (1925) 84, 145
New York Trilogy (1987) 103
Nietzsche, Friedrich (1844–1900) 81
Nolan, Christopher (1970–) 71
Norris, Frank (1870–1902) 67, 150
Notes from Underground (1864) 97

O'Connor, Flannery (1925–1964) 98, 105, 158
"Occurrence at Owl Creek Bridge, An" (1890) 70–71, 148
Octopus: A Story of California, The (1901) 67
Octoroon, The (1859) 51
"Ode on a Grecian Urn" (1820) 78
Odets, Clifford (1906–1963) 90
Of Plymouth Plantation (publ. 1856) 14
Oklahoma! (1943) 149
Old Man and the Sea, The (1951) 89
Olson, Charles (1910–1970) 96, 135
"On Being Brought from Africa to America" (1773) 25
"On the Relation of Analytical Psychology to Poetry" (1924) 116
On the Road (1951) 95, 134
O'Neill, Eugene (1888–1953) 84, 115, 141, 149
Orientalism (1978) 128
Our Town (1937) 91
"Over the fence" (publ. 1945) 58

Ovid (Publius Ovidus Naso) (43 BC–AD 17/18) 2
Ozick, Cynthia (1928–) 108

Pacino, Al (1940–) 95
Paine, Thomas (1737–1809) 28
Pale Fire (1962) 99, 154
Pale King, The (2011) 104
Pamela (1740) 31
Paradise Lost (1667) 119
Paris, Texas (1984) 95
Parmigianino (Girolamo Francesco Maria Mazzola) (1503–1540) 96
Passing (1929) 84
Peirce, Charles Sanders (1839–1914) 121, 157
Pelican Brief, The (1993) 95
"Perchance to Dream" (1996) 104
"Perfect Day for Bananafish, A" (1948) 99
"Personal Narrative of Jonathan Edwards" (publ. 1765) 24, 134
"Philosophy and the Form of Fiction" (1970) 103, 148
"Philosophy of Composition, The" (1846) 49, 113
Photoplay, The (1916) 117, 142
Picasso, Pablo (1881–1973) 72–73, 84, 137
"Pit and the Pendulum, The" (1842) 48
Pizarro, Francisco (*c.*1471 or 1476–1541) 6
Plath, Sylvia (1932–1963) 98
Plato (428/427–348/347 BC) 1
Pledge, The (2001) 95
Pocahontas (*c.*1595–1617) 12–13, 152

Poe, Edgar Allan (1809–1849) 33, 47–50, 71, 103–104, 113, 117–118, 133, 140, 148, 159–160
Poems on Various Subjects (1773) 25
"Poetic Principle, The" (1850) 113
Poitier, Sidney (1927–) 94
Polo, Marco (*c.*1254–1324) 1
Poor Richard's Almanack (1732–1758) 29
Portrait of a Lady, The (1881) 64
Postmodern Condition, The (1979) 153
Postmodernism (1991) 126
Pound, Ezra (1885–1972) 73–79, 85, 96, 110, 125, 135, 140, 144–145, 149, 151
Power of Sympathy, The (1789) 31, 157
Powhatan (*c.*1547–*c.*1618) 152
Preparatory Meditations (publ. 1939) 23
Price, Richard (1949–) 108, 110
Principles of Literary Criticism (1924) 116
"Projective Verse" (1950) 96, 135
"Protestant Ethic and the Spirit of Capitalism, The" (1904) 18, 154
Pulp Fiction (1994) 98
Pynchon, Thomas (1937–) 100–101, 103–104, 115, 153

Rabbit novels (1960–2001) 105
Raisin in the Sun, A (1959) 94
Raleigh, Sir Walter (*c.*1554–1618) 10, 12, 156, 161
Ransom, John Crowe (1888–1974) 119
"Raven, The" (1845) 49
Red Badge of Courage, The (1895) 66–67, 103

"Red Wheelbarrow, The" (1923) 78
Relación, La (1542) 6
"Resistance to Civil Government" (1849) 40
"Retrospect, A" (1918) 74
Rice, Elmer (1892–1967) 83, 141, 149
Richards, I. A. (1893–1979) 116, 119
Richardson, Samuel (1689–1761) 31
Riggs, Lynn (1899–1954) 149
"Rip van Winkle" (1819–1820) 34–35, 81
Rise of Silas Lapham, The (1885) 64
Rise of the Novel, The (1957) 126
Rockefeller, John D. (1839–1937) 60
Rorty, Richard (1931–2007) 123
Roth, Philip (1933–) 105, 108, 146
Rousseau and Romanticism (1919) 119
Rowlandson, Mary (*c.*1637–1711) 15, 134
Ruiz de Burton, María (1832–1895) 135

Said, Edward (1935–2003) 128
Salinger, J. D. (1919–2010) 47, 99–100, 115, 146
"Sandman, The" (1817) 116
Sarris, Andrew (1928–2012) 117, 134, 142
Saussure, Ferdinand de (1857–1913) 121, 123, 157
Scarlet Letter, The (1850) 42, 113
Scott, Sir Walter (1771–1732) 34–35
Sea Wolf, The (1904) 63
Self-Portrait in a Convex Mirror (1975) 96
"Self-Reliance" (1841) 38
Seven Types of Ambiguity (1930) 119

Sexual Perversity in Chicago (1974) 94
Shakespeare, William (1564–1616) 75–76, 81, 88, 126–127, 150
Shepard, Sam (1943–) 95, 110
Showalter, Elaine (1941–) 129
Shyamalan, M. Night (1970–) 48, 148
Sidney, Philip (1554–1586) 20, 112
Signifying Monkey, The (1988) 128
Silko, Leslie Marmon (1948–) 107, 150
Simpsons, The (1989–) 101
Singer, Isaac Bashevis (1902–1991) 108, 146
"Sinners in the Hands of an Angry God" (1741) 23, 136, 144–145
Sister Carrie (1900) 67
Sixth Sense, The (1999) 48, 71, 148
Sketch Book of Geoffrey Crayon, Gent., The (1819–1820) 34
Slaughterhouse-Five (1969) 102
Smith, John (*c*.1580–1631) 12–14, 146, 152
Sokal, Alan (1955–) 125
"Song of Myself" (1855) 54
Souls of Black Folk, The (1903) 84
Sound and the Fury, The (1929) 62, 88
Southern Literary Messenger (1834–1864) 47
Spenser, Edmund (*c*.1552–1599) 20
Spivak, Gayatri Chakravorty (1942–) 130
"Spontaneous Me" (1856) 55
St. John de Crèvecoeur, J. Hector (1735–1813) 27
Stanzel, Franz Karl (1923–) 66
Stein, Gertrude (1874–1946) 72–73, 76, 84, 90, 137, 149
Steinbeck, John (1902–1968) 90

Stevens, Wallace (1879–1955) 76–79
"Stopping by Woods on a Snowy Evening" (1920) 76
Stowe, Harriet Beecher (1811–1896) 50–51
Streetcar Named Desire, A (1947) 91
Sun Also Rises, The (1926) 89
Surprised by Sin (1967) 119
Swedenborg, Emanuel (1688–1772) 50

Tan, Amy (1952–) 108, 134
Tarantino, Quentin (1963–) 98
Tate, Allen (1899–1979) 119
Taylor, Edward (*c*.1644–1729) 22–23, 56, 79, 136
"Tell-Tale Heart, The" (1843) 47
Tempest, The (*c*.1611) 127
Tenney, Tabitha (1762–1837) 32, 151
Tenth Muse Lately Sprung up in America, The (1650) 21
Teseida (*c*.1339) 75
Their Eyes Were Watching God (1937) 84
Thoreau, Henry David (1817–1862) 37–41, 44, 46–47, 52, 55–56, 134, 160
Three Lives (1909) 73
"Tradition and the Individual Talent" (1920) 75
"Transgressing the Boundaries" (1996) 125
Trifles (1916) 82
True History of the Captivity and Restoration of Mrs. Mary Rowlandson, A (1682) 15
True West (1980) 95
Truffaut, François (1932–1984) 117, 134, 142

Turgenev, Ivan (1818–1883) 64
Twain, Mark (1835–1910) 63, 88, 143–144, 155, 159
Twin Peaks (1990–1991) 101
Typee (1846) 44–46

Ulysses (1922) 158
Uncle Tom's Cabin (1852) 50–51, 81
United States Bill of Rights (1789) 140
Updike, John (1932–2009) 105
U.S.A. Trilogy (1930–1936) 87, 158
Utopia (1515) 139, 161

Valdez, Luis (1940–) 107, 135
Vásquez de Coronado, Francisco (1510–1554) 6
Vendidos, Los (1967) 107, 135
"Verses upon the Burning of Our House, July 10th, 1666" (publ. 1678) 21
Vespucci, Amerigo (1452/54–1512) 3–4, 6, 139
"Visual Pleasure and Narrative Cinema" (1975) 117
Voice in the Closet, The (1979) 102
Voltaire (François-Marie Arouet) (1694–1778) 139
Vonnegut, Kurt (1922–2007) 102–103

Waiting for Godot (1952) 93, 160
Waiting for Lefty (1935) 90
Walden (1854) 38–40, 46, 134
Walker, Alice (1944–) 106
Wallace, David Foster (1962–2008) 104
Walpole, Horace (1717–1797) 32
Warner, Susan (1819–1858) 50
Washington, Booker T. (1856–1915) 84, 132, 145
Waste Land, The (1922) 75, 100, 154

Watt, Ian (1917–1999) 126
Weber, Max (1864–1920) 18, 29, 154
Webster, Noah (1758–1843) 28
Welles, Orson (1915–1985) 117
Wenders, Wim (1945–) 95
Wharton, Edith (1862–1937) 69–70, 155
Wheatley, Phillis (1753–1784) 24–26, 112, 132, 136
White, John (*c*.1540–1593) 9–10
Whitman, Walt (1819–1892) 52–56, 74, 95, 113, 160
Who's Afraid of Virginia Woolf? (1962) 93
Wide, Wide World, The (1850) 50
Wilder, Thornton (1897–1975) 91
Williams, Raymond (1921–1988) 127, 137
Williams, Roger (1603–1683) 15, 19
Williams, Tennessee (1911–1983) 91–92
Williams, William Carlos (1883–1963) 76, 78–79
Wilson, Woodrow (1856–1924) 87
Wimsatt, William K. (1907–1975) 119
Winthrop, John (1588–1649) 18, 136, 145
Wire, The (2002–2008) 108
Wolfe, Tom (1931–) 105
Woman in the Nineteenth Century (1845) 41, 129, 141
Woman Warrior, The (1975) 108
Women and Economics (1898) 68, 129
Wonders of the Invisible World, The (1693) 19
Wordsworth, William (1770–1850) 156

Wright, Richard (1908–1960) 106, 132

"Yellow Wallpaper, The" (1890) 68, 83

Zabriskie Point (1970) 95
Zola, Émile (1840–1902) 64
Zoo Story, The (1958) 93–94, 160
Zuckerman novels (1974–2007) 108

Subject index

affective fallacy 120, 132, 150
African-American literature 24–25, 51–52, 84–85, 106–107, 128, 132, 140, 144, 157
alienation effect 91, 133
American Renaissance 44–59, 133
archetypal criticism 81, 116, 133
Asian-American literature 106–108, 128, 133–134, 140
Atlantis 1
auteur theory 117, 134, 142
author-oriented approaches 115–118, 120, 129, 131, 134, 142, 150
authorial self-reflection 112
autobiography 15, 24, 29–30, 38–40, 43, 47, 51–52, 115, 134, 149, 158
Aztec empire 6

Beat Generation 55, 95, 134
biographical criticism 115
Black Mountain School 96, 135

Chicano/Chicana literature 106–107, 128, 135, 140
Chinese ideogram 74, 135
close reading 120, 135–136, 150

Colonial or Puritan Age 10–26, 28, 110, 131–132, 136
conceit 22–23, 56–57, 59, 76, 79, 136, 148, 151
concrete poetry 58, 76, 79, 101, 136
context-oriented approach 125–131, 137
cubism 72–73, 84, 102, 137, 149
cultural studies 127, 137

Declaration of Independence 28–29, 41, 136–139
deconstruction 123–126, 128, 130–131, 137–138, 150, 152, 159, 161
detective fiction 48–50, 103, 118, 159
différance 123–124, 138
discourse 126–127, 139, 149–150
discovery and travel narratives 1–9, 139

Early Republic 27–36, 131, 139–140
écriture féminine 130, 141, 143
enlightenment 24, 28–30, 138–140, 144, 156
epic 75–76, 110, 119, 140

Subject index

epistolary novel 31, 140
ethnic voices 106–111, 140
expressionism 81–83, 141

feminism 41, 43, 67–69, 82, 91, 94, 98, 108, 129–130, 141, 143
feminist literary theory 67–69, 82, 84, 89, 117, 128–130, 137, 141, 143
figural narrative situation 65, 142, 149
film theory 116–117, 122–123, 134, 142–143, 154
first-person narration 45–46, 48, 61, 65, 85, 96, 98–100, 104, 140, 143, 149
formalism 114, 119, 121, 142–143, 150, 158–159, 161
Frankfurt School 126, 143
French feminism 129–130, 143
frontier literature 15, 23, 26, 35, 110, 139, 151

gender theory 83, 89, 128, 130–131, 141, 143, 153
Gilded Age 60–69, 144
Golden Age 2, 5
Gothic novel 32–33, 48, 112, 144
Great Awakening 23–24, 144
Great Depression 85, 87, 145–146

haiku 74, 135, 144–145
Harlem Renaissance 84, 85, 132, 144–145
historical novel 35
homiletic prose 18, 145

images of women criticism 129, 141
imagism 74, 76, 114, 135, 144–145, 149, 151
implied reader 118, 145

Incan empire 6
intentional fallacy 120, 146, 150

Jamestown 12–13, 146, 152
Jazz Age 85, 87, 146
Jewish-American literature 108, 146

literary theory 112–131, 142, 147, 159, 161

manifest destiny 147
Marxist literary theory 125–126, 131, 137, 143, 147
Massachusetts Bay Colony 18–20, 152
Mayflower 14, 147
Mayflower Compact 14, 147
McCarthy era 20, 92, 147
metafiction 35, 93, 100–103, 108, 148, 153
Metaphysical poets 22, 56, 59, 75–76, 79, 136, 148, 151
mind-tricking narratives 48, 71, 148
modernism 58–60, 62, 67, 69–93, 96, 110, 114, 131, 137, 144, 148–149, 154
mulatto drama 51

narrative perspective 61–62, 65–66, 77, 85, 88, 97, 142, 148–149, 158
narratology 66, 123, 142, 149
Native-American literature 106–107, 140, 149–150
Native Americans 2–13, 15–17, 19–20, 33, 35–36, 140, 146–147, 149, 151–152, 156
naturalism 64, 66–67, 88, 94, 110, 150

New Criticism 49, 56, 113–114, 118–121, 124, 131–132, 135, 146, 150, 159, 161
New Historicism 126–127, 131, 137, 139, 150
New Humanism 114, 151
noble savage 2, 5, 13, 46, 151
northwest passage 7, 9
novel of manners 65, 110, 155

objective correlative 75, 79–80, 151
omniscient or authorial narrative situation 151

paradise 2, 3, 5, 10, 139
picaresque novel 32, 151
Pilgrim Fathers 14, 18, 147, 152
Plymouth Colony 14–17, 136, 152
Pocahontas myth 12, 151–152
postcolonial literature 128, 152
postcolonial theory 128, 152
postmodernism 47, 58–59, 93–105, 148, 153–154, 159
poststructuralism 121, 124–128, 138, 150, 152–153, 161
predestination 15, 17–18, 22, 144, 153–154
primary and secondary literature 75, 100, 104, 123, 154
Protestant work ethic 18, 29, 40, 47, 83, 90, 154
psychoanalytic literary theory 59, 113, 115–117, 120, 131, 150, 154
psychological film theory 116–117, 142, 154
Puritan interregnum 19, 155
Puritanism, Puritans 14–19, 22–23, 28–30, 47, 56, 59, 81, 83, 110, 134, 136, 144, 147, 152–155, 157

queer theory 130

reader-oriented approaches 118–119, 121, 131, 147, 155
reader-response theory 118, 155
realism 60–70, 88, 90, 110, 113–114, 131, 141, 144, 150, 155–156
"red thirties" 87, 90
Roanoke or the Lost Colony 11, 156
roman à clef 43, 98, 156
romance 41, 43, 64, 113, 156
romanticism 35, 37–38, 48, 76–78, 156

Salem witchcraft trials 20, 42, 92, 157
semiotics 121–122, 127, 138, 142, 157, 159
sentimental novel 31–32, 50, 139, 157
Separatists 14, 152
signifier and signified 121, 123, 131, 138, 157
slave narratives 51–52, 132, 157
Southern Gothic 98, 158
stream-of-consciousness technique 87, 92, 142, 149, 158
structuralism and formalism 119, 124, 127, 138, 143, 153, 158–159, 161
surrealism 60, 79

tales of ratiocination 48–49, 148, 159
tall tale 61, 159
text-oriented approaches 119–125, 129, 143, 147, 150, 155, 158–159

theater of the absurd 47, 84, 93–94, 99, 153, 159
transcendentalism 37–43, 50, 52, 62, 67, 77, 110, 156–157, 160

"understanding" vs. "reason" dichotomy 40, 46, 160
unity of effect 49, 113, 140, 160
utopian literature 1, 26, 69, 139, 161

Virginia Charter 10, 156
Virginia Company 12, 14, 147, 152

war fiction 103

Yale Critics 124, 138, 161
"yuppie novel" 104

For Product Safety Concerns and Information please contact our EU
representative GPSR@taylorandfrancis.com
Taylor & Francis Verlag GmbH, Kaufingerstraße 24, 80331 München, Germany

www.ingramcontent.com/pod-product-compliance
Lightning Source LLC
Chambersburg PA
CBHW070258230426
43664CB00014B/2576